The Buzz About *WORLD WAR BRANDS*

"*WORLD WAR BRANDS* is an entertaining and enlightening story of the beginning of disciplined marketing and advertising in America. The extent of Barry Silverstein's research is incredible – he shares, displays, reports and comments on the many brands of the era. The treasure in the book is the pictorial collection of ads that were placed during the war, capturing the focus of America at that time. This book is well organized, easy to read and an informative, nostalgic journey through classic brands and World War II realities."
Peter W. Evans, Retired Advertising Agency President

"This impressively researched and fascinating book reveals how brand destinies are shaped not only by culture and technology but by global events. From Ray-Ban aviator sunglasses and Donald Duck to Cocoa Puffs and Car Culture, Barry Silverstein explains how American brands responded to World War II and – despite its human toll – went on to create a vibrant post-war consumer society and lay the foundations of modern marketing."
Barry Robertson, Partner
Boomer / next division of VizioNation, a generational marketing consultancy

"Anyone interested in American history and America's most successful brands will find *WORLD WAR BRANDS* an enlightening read. Barry Silverstein does a great job summarizing how America was changing from 1920 through the 1960s and how America's best-known brands evolved in response. This is a highly worthwhile read for the marketing or brand history enthusiast."
Francis J. Kelly III, President and CEO
CEOVIEW Branding LLC

"...Silverstein is keenly aware of the centrality of branding to 20th-century advertising. Three dozen print-ad reproductions complement the book's engaging writing style... Overall, it's a convincing history about the role of World War II in developing brand consciousness among consumers in the United States."
Kirkus Reviews

WORLD WAR BRANDS

World War II and the Rise of the Modern American Brand

Barry Silverstein

GuideWords Publishing

Copyright © 2021 by Barry Silverstein

All rights reserved.

No part of this publication may be reproduced without written permission from the publisher except in cases of fair use. Contact the publisher for permissions use. The author and publisher have made every effort to ensure that the information in this publication is correct; however, neither author nor publisher will accept any liability to any party for any loss, damage, or disruption caused by errors or omissions, whether such errors or omissions result from negligence, accident, or any other cause. The opinions expressed are solely those of the author.

All trademarks and registered trademarks are the property of their respective holders.

Website links are accurate as of the time of publication and are subject to change.

GuideWords Publishing
5 Blue Damsel Court
Biltmore Lake, NC 28715 USA
www.guidewordspub.com

Cover Design by Charala
Book Layout © 2017 BookDesignTemplates.com

World War Brands – Barry Silverstein -- 1st ed.
Library of Congress Control Number 2021900376
Paperbound edition ISBN 978-0-9965760-8-6
eBook edition ISBN 978-0-9965760-9-3

Printed in the United States of America

Contents

Introduction: World War II and American Brands — 7

PART I – The American Brand: World War I to World War II

Chapter 1: How the U.S. Government Branded the Great War — 15

Chapter 2: How American Brands Leveraged the Great War — 23

Chapter 3: American Brands in the 1920s — 31

Chapter 4: American Brands in the 1930s — 37

PART II – The American Brand and World War II

Chapter 5: At War: Advertising and the U.S. Government — 43

Chapter 6: World War Brands — 59

Chapter 7: The Dark Side of World War Brands — 109

PART III – The Birth of the Modern American Brand

Chapter 8: The Consumer in Post-War America — 131

Chapter 9: The Era of Television — 145

Chapter 10: The Modern Brand is Born — 185

Afterword: The Brand Moves On — 197

Sources — 199

Appendix: Print Ads — 229

Brand Index — 307

About the Author — 317

• INTRODUCTION •

World War II and American Brands

I was born in 1948, a few years after the end of World War II, so I didn't experience it first-hand. Still, my father was a medical doctor in the war and he had many stories to tell. Like other boys who grew up in the Fifties, I was simultaneously fascinated and horrified by World War II. I saw the outcome from an American perspective – good decisively defeating evil.

I didn't think much about the war in adulthood. I spent my professional career doing marketing programs for brands. I've written several books about brands; in two of those books, I chronicled brands of the 1950s and 1960s that appealed to my generation – I called them "Boomer Brands." In considering how those brands originated, I began to wonder what role World War II might have played in influencing their rise.

As I researched the interrelationship of World War II and American brands, I realized that branding took on a broader meaning. World War II itself was "branded" by the American government in association with American brand advertisers, who collectively and aggressively promoted war bonds, victory gardens and patriotism throughout the war years. In fact, there was a financial incentive offered by the U.S. government to do so. Radio, newspapers, magazines, posters and film were painstakingly coordinated in a media campaign designed to disseminate government sponsored war-related messages – in reality war propaganda – often supported by specific brands. It was quite a remarkable branding effort. It turns out that this wasn't the first time America branded a war: The American government and business had done this before, during World War I (also known as the Great War). But they perfected their partnership in World War II.

World War II had a profound impact on American brands. In addition to brands directly aligning their products with the war effort, some brands, such as Coca-Cola, used the war as a clever way to engender positive perceptions by distributing their products to American forces. Other brands actually had their roots in the war. For example, M&Ms were introduced in 1941 for soldiers; they were designed with a hard candy outer shell so the chocolate inside wouldn't melt on the battlefield. Early on, M&Ms were used exclusively by the American military before they were widely available to consumers. Jeeps became synonymous with American ground forces. The jeep was as essential a piece of military equipment as boots and weapons. "Jeep" grew directly out of its military use to become an automobile brand. Both brands, M&Ms and Jeep, remain as popular today as during the World War II era.

Just as important, the post-war economy led to the rise of the American middle class. The war fueled strong economic growth that turned the country into a major global force. Americans were thrilled to break out of wartime frugality; they enthusiastically adopted the role of materialistic consumers. They were ready, willing and able to purchase a wide range of consumer products. Manufacturers were happy to oblige; the result was that post-war America became a bubbling cauldron of scores of inventive, innovative brands. When television came along, marketing those brands rose to a whole new level.

This book is about both the branding of World War II and the impact the war had on the modern American brand. I intend for it to be informal and hopefully entertaining rather than a scholarly study. I approach the subject as a marketing professional, not a credentialed historian. Unlike other World War II books, this book doesn't focus on the reasons for war or the war itself; rather, it presents an exploration of the interplay between World War II and American brands. It examines American brands historically, from right before to right after World War II. In so doing, I hope to make a compelling case that World War II greatly contributed to the rise of the modern American brand.

How This Book is Organized

1. Part I lays the groundwork for my thesis. It is an overview of the American brand between World War I and World War II. This section is a kind of preamble that reflects on brands and their role in popular culture prior to World War II. It will be apparent that the Great War was "branded," and American brands played a role in marketing the war.

2. Part II covers the branding of World War II. I discuss the primary media and techniques that were used by the American government and American brands to support the war effort and spread propaganda about the war. The heart of the book presents how American brands marketed themselves during World War II. Here, you'll see how specific brands integrated their marketing message with the war, and how some brands used the war to increase their own product awareness and sales. I also discuss the dark side of war brands – both American and foreign brands that collaborated with the enemy. Some of the brands we know today emerged as market leaders during this time, while others have been relegated to the dustbin of history.

3. Part III addresses brands in the context of American post-war culture, moving from the war's end into the 1950s and 1960s. This part demonstrates how the consumerism of post-war America led quite directly to the birth of breakthrough brands and modern brand

marketing strategies, helped along by a major media development called television. Many brands from this time have survived and thrived into the 21st Century. If you're over sixty-five years of age, you are likely to remember a number of these brands and their catchy television jingles from your childhood. If you're younger, you will probably get a kick out of discovering how brands that continue to be vibrant today really got their start.

4. The Appendix contains numerous print ads from the World War II era. Each ad is numbered. The text will reference an ad in the Appendix by its number like this: (*Appendix, 1*).

If you want to learn more about the branding aspects of World War II or the many brands covered in this book, check out the Sources section for weblinks to additional information. Also included in that section are links to some of the original television commercials for brands referenced in the book.

I hope you enjoy this journey into an intriguing period of American history that I call "World War Brands."

Note: All company and brand trademarks and registered trademarks referenced in this book are the property of their respective holders.

• PART I •

The American Brand: World War I to World War II

• CHAPTER 1 •

How the U.S. Government Branded the Great War

America's involvement in World War I (known at the time as the "Great War") was anything but a foregone conclusion. The war was viewed by Americans as a European conflict when it began in 1914. President Woodrow Wilson was committed to American neutrality early on. The turning point in how Americans perceived the war probably came in May 1915, when the British passenger ship *Lusitania* was attacked by German U-boats. On board were Americans, over 120 of whom died in the sinking of the ship. That brought the war perilously close to home in the minds of many Americans.

Even so, Wilson was hesitant to join the Allies in combat. As he ran again in 1916, Wilson stressed America's "preparedness" and employed the campaign slogan, "He Kept Us Out of War." Apparently, this is what Americans wanted to hear –Woodrow Wilson was re-elected. But the second-term president's assurance didn't last long. When German submarines attacked American vessels and it was discovered that Germany attempted to cajole Mexico into becoming its war ally, the United States entered the war in April 1917.

Once the war began, the majority of Americans were in favor of it. Over one million men enlisted in the armed forces, as did about twenty thousand women. "Selective service" was instituted and most men who were drafted joined the military willingly.

As soon as America became engaged in the Great War, the "Committee on Public Information" (CPI) was formed by the federal government to brand the war in a positive light, spread patriotic propaganda and drum up support for the war across the country. To ensure that Americans remained loyal to the war effort, Wilson bolstered the CPI with legal penalties for dissension through the Espionage and Sedition Acts. The stage was set for American businesses, organizations, institutions and the public to rally around the country – and rally they did.

The CPI reported directly to Wilson and was headed by George Creel, a former newspaperman. Notable writers and artists of the era worked on behalf of the CPI, including:
- Edward Bernays, who leveraged his war experience to eventually become recognized as the father of modern public relations
- Charles Dana Gibson, an artist who created the famous "Gibson Girl" illustrations

- Walter Lippmann, who later became a renowned political commentator
- Norman Rockwell, a young illustrator who would grow into one of the most beloved American artists
- Ida Tarbell, a prominent muckraking journalist
- Novelist Booth Tarkington
- Newspaper editor William Allen White.

The CPI marshaled the forces of both government and private industry to create what was essentially the most pervasive, sophisticated American brand marketing campaign to date. Employing every medium available, along with the extensive use of talks, speeches and elaborate exhibitions, the CPI set out an ambitious goal to communicate with and influence all American citizens with the message that supporting the American war effort was everyone's patriotic duty. The CPI penetrated virtually all publicly available venues, also engaging Hollywood filmmakers to produce patriotic movies that were widely shown. The CPI was even empowered to work with the U.S. Postal Service to root out and censor negative propaganda against the war.

One of the more effective mediums of the time was the poster, previously used only for advertising products. Banks, post offices and local businesses with storefronts willingly displayed patriotic posters that were produced by the U. S. government as well as private firms. America followed the lead of Great Britain, relying on posters to recruit for the military, promote the sale of war bonds and encourage women to support the war at home through such organizations as the Red Cross and the YWCA.

Arguably the most famous poster of the Great War is one depicting "Uncle Sam," accompanied by the slogan, "I WANT YOU FOR U.S. ARMY." (*Appendix, 1*) This poster personified the nation in the form of an older gent in patriotic dress who had a serious expression and sternly pointed his finger at the viewer.

The poster was illustrated by James Montgomery Flagg, a colorful high-spirited man who wanted to support the war effort but, at age thirty-nine, couldn't enlist in the armed forces because he was too old. Flagg actually used himself as the model for Uncle Sam – he applied makeup that included a fake goatee, wore a top hat and looked into a mirror to create the iconic image from his reflection. Four million copies of the recruitment poster were printed, and Flagg's "Uncle Sam" character continued to be used on other posters and in published materials to support the war. In fact, Uncle Sam's popularity never flagged – when World War II came along, the Great War recruitment poster was resurrected and put to use a second time.

Other posters targeted specific audiences with unique messages. One poster, for example, showed an illustration of a little boy saluting, along with a bowl of cereal. The poster made the point that wheat was valuable and needed to be preserved for the war effort. The text read:

Little AMERICANS
Do your bit
Eat Corn meal mush –
Oatmeal – Corn flakes
Hominy and rice with
milk. *Eat no wheat
cereals.*
Leave nothing on your plate

Whether it was posters, leaflets, advertisements in newspapers and magazines, films or speeches, the CPI was omnipotent. Just imagine a brand advertiser with a virtually unlimited budget who could convey a strong, unified message multiple times to over 103 million people (about the number of individuals in the U.S. in 1917). That was the awesome power of the Committee on Public Information. In his book about World War I propaganda, *How We Advertised America*, George Creel boasted that the CPI was "the world's greatest adventure in advertising."

Still, consider the enormous challenge Wilson and the CPI faced from a branding perspective. One of the most difficult things any brand marketer can do is *change a perception*. It is often stated in psychology that "perception is reality." In this case, Wilson needed to change the perception, or the reality in the minds of most Americans, that the United States was an *isolationist*. Instead, Wilson needed to convince people that the country should become an *interventionist*. This new brand position for the country was essential if Wilson was to gain support for a war he previously said was unnecessary in which to engage.

Changing the perception of the U.S. role in the war had to be done quickly – as soon as the United States entered the conflict. That's why the CPI was formed, why it secured such a skilled group of communicators and why it did not hesitate to immediately spread messages emphasizing patriotism and nationalism in order to brand and "sell" the war to Americans.

Not all of the propaganda was noble – some of the less savory messaging concentrated on and even exaggerated the brutality of the opposition. Labeled "atrocity propaganda," advertising featuring war acts of unspeakable savagery by Austrians and Germans was not uncommon. Abhorrent imagery was often highlighted in both incendiary words and graphic illustrations to justify going to war against a cruel, heartless enemy. The CPI may not have publicly condoned the use of such negative propaganda, but the committee apparently did not prevent its dissemination. One side effect of atrocity propaganda was to foster intolerance and foment hatred of German immigrants living in America.

Some advertisers took advantage of atrocity propaganda in a commercial way. For example, a 1917 ad placed by the *New York Tribune*, a newspaper of the time, promoted excerpts from a diary written by an American official. The ad depicted a huge hand grasping a woman with the headline, "The RAPE of BELGIUM." Accompanying text read, "A day by day record of the German's drive through Belgium – a narrative of fact.

Dramatic – thrilling – true! Start reading it to-day. Daily and Sunday in the New York Tribune."

Other ads, disparaging the enemy but somewhat less inflammatory, tied directly into product promotion. In Great Britain, an ad for Decca, "The Portable Gramophone," featured the headline, "The cussed Huns have got my gramophone." According to the ad, "The 'Decca' is the ideal gramophone for Active Service. It can be carried with ease anywhere. No case required; no loose parts to get lost. Plays perfectly all makes and sizes of needle records."

Regardless, the marketing of the Great War to the American public was a rousing success – so much so that it found its way right into the homes of American families. Since radio was not yet commercialized and television was not yet available, gathering the family around a piano to sing songs was popular at the time. A 1917 ad in *The Saturday Evening Post* offered an 80-page book, "Songs The Soldiers and Sailors Sing," featuring "Songs that reach from Here to 'Over There.'" A majority of songs copyrighted in 1918 were patriotic war songs, and sheet music often had pro-war illustrations on the cover. You might say that the Great War was very much in tune with the sentiment of ordinary Americans.

• CHAPTER 2 •

How American Brands Leveraged the Great War

The relationship between American brands and the federal government during the Great War was complex. An organization called the War Industries Board was formed to help coordinate governmental needs with industry. Branches of the military sometimes competed with each other in procuring raw materials and the products they required for combat. Manufacturers provided products to help the war effort, yet they had to also protect their domestic supply chains. Manufacturers who didn't cooperate could find themselves restricted by the government from receiving the materials they needed to make products for consumers.

In 1917, American brand advertising was coming into its own – the American Association of Advertising Agencies was founded that year. When it came to marketing, American brands and their agencies quickly recognized that advertising their products in collaboration with promoting the Great War was a winning proposition in more ways than one. Such an alignment allowed brands to boast about their commitment to patriotism and show consumers they supported the war effort. The advertising division of the CPI offered paid sponsorships to businesses so their names could appear on war marketing paraphernalia and be associated with the sale of war bonds, food appeals and fuel conservation.

There was a cultural aspect to the way American brands advertised during the Great War. While patriotism, nationalism and military superiority were openly promoted, so too were messages related to specific products advertised on the home front. The automobile industry is a good example. Automobiles were expensive, but they represented the up-and-coming mode of transportation. Still, automobile manufacturers wanting to advertise their new models had to be sensitive to the war effort. One ad from the Electric Vehicle Company was way ahead of its time when it appeared in 1917. The ad showed an illustration of a car and read: "LADIES, BE PATRIOTIC – drive your own DETROIT ELECTRIC and avoid the use of gasoline, oil and chauffeurs, now needed by the government."

Cosmetics products focused on the emerging role of the woman as a worker who replaced men going off to war. As such, brand advertisers wanted to convey that it was important for the woman to care for herself and regain her femininity and appearance when she returned home after a hard day's work devoted to the war effort. For example, the headline of a 1917 magazine ad for Pompeian Night Cream promised, "Sleep and

Grow Beautiful." The text went on, "Many a woman loses her good looks by losing an hour or so of precious sleep every night. Sleep is indeed nature's great beautifier. To make youthful beauty linger in your face, get more sleep and form the habit of *nightly* use of a good cream."

Some brand marketers took advantage of the war to directly promote their products to consumers as if buying them was an act of patriotism. A 1917 ad from the Gillette Safety Razor Co. showed an illustration of an army soldier and a navy sailor accompanied by the headline, "Gillette U.S. Service Set. It Fits the Kit or the Pocket." The ad copy began with the text, "Here is how the Great War developed the most compact and efficient shaving outfit in the world." The ad went on to promote a $5 shaving kit for soldiers, packaged in "a solid metal case, heavy nickel-plated and embossed with the Insignia of the U.S. Army and Navy." The ad continued, "You ought to see the boys reach for them! Every man in Khaki ought to have one."

Other brand marketers incorporated the government's war rationing messages into their ads – even if the connection wasn't all that obvious. In a 1918 ad, Lucky Strike cigarettes featured the headline, "Use OYSTERS Instead of MEAT." The text of the ad continued, "The Food Administration says so. And broiled oysters! In their shells; savory, juicy – a strip of bacon on each. What a delicious taste! Let's go! You'll find that cooking does as much for the taste of tobacco. Try Lucky Strike cigarettes – it's toasted." This ad played upon Lucky Strike's advertising slogan, "It's toasted."

Brand marketers didn't ignore the fighting man, either. In *The Stars and Stripes*, a newspaper that targeted the military, American companies unabashedly integrated patriotism with product marketing. Chewing gum and cigarettes were staples of American soldiers, so these brands frequently advertised in the newspaper:

- An ad for Wrigley's chewing gum published in 1918 showed a picture of army and navy servicemen with the text, "The use of WRIGLEY'S by the fighting men has created much comment in war correspondence. Even before American soldiers and sailors landed, the British, Canadian and French forces had adopted WRIGLEY'S as their wartime sweetmeat. And now that Uncle Sam's stalwart boys are hitting the line, WRIGLEY'S is a very noticeable ally of the Allies."

- Fatima cigarettes, a product of Liggett & Myers Tobacco Co., ran an ad in 1919 that stated, "A fact: Among the thousands of physicians and surgeons, from all sections of the United States, in training at Fort Riley, Kansas, for Army service, it turned out that Fatimas far and away outsold every other cigarette – day in and day out. That fact speaks for itself."

A final interesting footnote to brand marketing during World War I: There were products that the American consumer enjoyed in later years as a direct result of the Great War. Here are some examples:

The Trench Coat

One lasting influence of the war on fashion was the **trench coat**, developed to repel the rain and the chill of the open trenches. Thomas Burberry designed a trench coat for the British army in the early 1900s. The trench coat was worn by British officers in the Great War, although Aquascutum, another British clothing manufacturer, claimed to develop a similar coat as early as the 1850s. It was Burberry, though, that popularized the trench coat with consumers in Great Britain and later in America.

On the trench coat, as in other clothing, buttons were the closures of choice in the early 1900s. In 1913, a "hookless fastener" was developed by Gideon Sundback, a Swedish-born engineer who worked for the Universal Fastener Company. He received a patent in 1917, just in time for the product to be appropriated for the Great War. The newly patented fastener was used in place of buttons to keep the money belts of soldiers and sailors closed, and later by aviators for securing their flying suits. That fastener was renamed the "zipper" by B. F. Goodrich Company in 1923. Goodrich used the zipper on boots; by the 1930s, the zipper was being incorporated into consumer clothing.

The Wristwatch

Men used **pocket watches** before the war and women wore wristwatches as fashion accessories. In the late 1800s, however, a naval officer rigged up a wristband for his pocket watch and the idea spread. By the Second Boer War (1899 – 1902), sturdy watches on wristbands were worn by those in combat. In the

United States, the pocket watch was still a man's preferred mode of time-telling in the early 1900s, but during the Great War, a pocket watch was impractical; officers and aviators started wearing wristwatches to keep their hands free. That custom cemented the popularity of men's wristwatches in the U.S.

Stainless Steel
Stainless steel began as a metal developed in 1913 in Great Britain by Harry Brearley, who mixed chromium and iron to produce a steel impervious to rust. Reportedly, Brearley was trying to prevent British gun barrels from rusting when the Great War started. While stainless steel proved to be less than optimum for weapons, it was used during the war to make aircraft engines, medical instruments and mess kit eating utensils. After the war, stainless steel became widely used in the U.S. to manufacture silverware. By the 1930s, stainless steel was used to make trains, aircraft and kitchen sinks.

Kotex and Kleenex
A women's hygiene product and the best-known brand of tissues were outgrowths of the Great War. With cotton in short supply, Kimberly-Clark developed "Cellucotton," a material made from wood pulp that was more absorbent and less expensive than cotton. The American military first used it for surgical dressings. Then ingenious Red Cross nurses discovered another use for the material – sanitary pads. After the war, Kimberly-Clark bought back surplus Cellucotton from the military. In the

1920s, the company turned it into two consumer products: **Kotex sanitary pads** and **Kleenex tissues** (*Appendix*, 2). Both brands still exist today. Despite "Kleenex" being a trademarked name, it is commonly used by consumers as a noun to replace the word "tissues," probably to the dismay of the brand's owner, Kimberly-Clark.

• CHAPTER 3 •

American Brands in the 1920s

The post-war era held enormous promise for American brands, but there was an uneasy interlude between the victorious end of the Great War in late 1918 and the beginning of a new decade. The year 1918 was marred by the onset of the deadliest modern flu pandemic in history, called the "Spanish Flu." It first affected American soldiers and then spread throughout the country and the world. A spate of ads promoting flu-related remedies, virtually all unsubstantiated, appeared in newspapers and magazines.

In 1919, the flu pandemic was still raging, although it finally abated by the summer. The American economy was in transition. Manufacturing firms were under siege by workers who wanted to benefit from a return to peacetime. Schisms between whites and Blacks, along with intolerance for immigrants, Catholics and Jews, fueled societal unrest and rioting.

Even with the turbulence, Americans were optimistic about the future. The country roared into the Twenties with a dual personality: On the one hand, the American consumer was ready to have fun again, anxious to leave the war and pandemic behind and spend money on "the good things in life." It was an era of Flappers, talking movies, a woman's right to vote and conspicuous consumption. An African American migration from the South to the North helped to drive the popularity of jazz.

On the other hand, discrimination against Blacks and fear of "Communist" immigrants continued to flare, political corruption was common and organized crime was rampant. One reaction to this social upheaval was temperance, resulting in the national prohibition of alcohol ("Prohibition"). Unfortunately, this legislation only served to drive drinking underground.

Brands re-entered the post-war economy with a new vitality, having learned from the enormous branding campaign conducted on behalf of the war itself. Brands had the opportunity to advertise in major newspapers and national magazines, including a new periodical that would become very popular, *TIME*. Radio, an emerging medium, was still in its commercial infancy, but radio receivers were entrenched in seventeen percent of American households by the middle of the decade. Radio would eventually prove to be fertile ground for brand advertisers by the early 1930s.

While some brand marketers continued to make wild, unsubstantiated claims for such products as patent medicines, brand advertising in general began to mature as ad agencies embraced a more sophisticated approach focused on practical, measurable advertising. Mail order ads and direct mail catalogs were increasingly popular. *Scientific Advertising* by Claude Hopkins, the classic book that pioneered results-driven marketing, was published in 1923.

New retail chains and American companies across many industry segments were formed in the 1920s, reflecting the growth of a consumer-oriented marketplace. These companies included:

- Ace Hardware
- Birds Eye
- Carvel
- Chrysler
- CVS
- Delta Air Lines
- Hasbro
- Howard Johnson's
- Lowe's
- Metro Goldwyn Mayer
- Pan American Airways
- Radio Shack
- Rubbermaid
- Schick
- 7-Eleven
- Thom McAn
- The Walt Disney Company
- Wise Foods

Products that appealed to the consumer's self-interest were especially popular. Brands in industry sectors such as automobiles, cigarettes, clothing, entertainment, personal care and snack foods were prominent. Here are some brand examples from each category:

Automobiles
Ford

Automobiles were mostly a luxury item for rich people until Henry Ford came along. Ford developed techniques to mass-produce American automobiles. The first notable Ford brand, the Model T, was sold as early as 1909, but the car reached the height of its popularity in the 1920s. It was so affordable that a majority of Americans eventually owned at least one automobile. More than fifteen million Model T automobiles were manufactured between 1913 and 1927, when the car was discontinued.

Cigarettes
Lucky Strike

Even before the Great War, cigarettes were popular with American men. Cigarette brands began to proliferate in the 1920s; among them were Camel, Chesterfield, Old Gold and Lucky Strike. Using the slogan, "It's Toasted," Lucky Strike made heavy use of print and radio for brand advertising. The brand was an early sponsor of music programs on radio, such as "B. A. Rolfe and his Lucky Strike Orchestra," and continued radio advertising in the 1930s, sponsoring "Your Hit Parade." Part of Lucky Strike's success was attributed to its advertising directed to women in the late 1920s. By 1930, Lucky Strike was the leading national cigarette brand.

Clothing
Chanel

One of the most notable and enduring brand names in fashion is Chanel, founded by French fashion designer Gabrielle "Coco" Chanel. While her early ambition was to be a stage entertainer, that didn't work out, so Chanel transitioned to fashion. In 1921, she opened one of the first fashion boutiques in Paris. Chanel is credited with designing the "little black dress" in 1926. She also broke through design conventions with her pants and suits designed for women. Her iconic perfume, "Chanel No. 5" was popular in department stores by the mid-20s.

Entertainment
MGM

Moving pictures flourished during the 1920s, when most major film studios were born. Three film companies were merged in 1924 to form Metro-Goldwyn-Mayer, later known as MGM. The MGM brand was recognized nationally by movie theater audiences because of a lion that appeared at the start of each film (but the lion was silent and didn't roar until 1928). At a time when Hollywood stars were under contract to studios, MGM boasted the mega-stars Clark Gable, Greta Garbo and Spencer Tracy. Among its many well-known early films were *The Big Parade* (1925), *Broadway Melody* (1929), *Mutiny on the Bounty* (1935) and *Gone with the Wind* (1939).

Personal Care
Palmolive

Of the numerous soap brands popular in the 1920s, none surpassed Palmolive (*Appendix, 3*), whose name was a combination of Palm and Olive oils. Created in 1898, Palmolive was the best-selling soap in the world by the early 1900s. In the Twenties, the brand wanted to keep up with the times, so it introduced a new slogan, "Keep that Schoolgirl Complexion," to appeal to the modern-day woman. While the maker of Palmolive merged with Colgate in 1928, the Palmolive brand is still being sold today.

Snack Foods
Baby Ruth

The snack food category of the 1920s was populated by chewing gum and candy. The candy bar Baby Ruth (*Appendix, 4*) was introduced in 1920 and became the best-selling 5-cent candy bar by the end of the decade. Made of peanuts, caramel and chocolate, Baby Ruth's popularity is sometimes overshadowed by the hotly contested dispute over the origin of its name. To this day, there are claims that it was named in honor of (1) President Grover Cleveland's daughter Ruth (2) candy maker George Williamson's granddaughter Ruth or (3) baseball player Babe Ruth, who was famous at the time. Regardless, the Curtiss Candy Company promoted the candy cleverly: During the 1920s, the company dropped thousands of Baby Ruth bars onto American city streets via tiny parachutes. In 1929, Curtiss sponsored a CBS radio program called "The Baby Ruth Hour."

• CHAPTER 4 •

American Brands in the 1930s

The beginning of the 1930s was an even worse moment in history than the turmoil leading into the 1920s. In October 1929, the stock market crash marked the start of the Great Depression, which lasted well into the 1930s. By 1931, six million Americans were out of work and by 1933 thousands of banks had failed. A seriously depressed economy caused the collapse of consumer buying. Advertising agencies, already suffering from a negative image because of the unsubstantiated claims of the previous decade, had to both repair the reputation of their industry and convince advertisers to invest during the Depression.

Newspapers and magazines continued to dominate media, but by 1932, print publications were under competitive pressure from radio. Two radio networks, CBS and NBC, made it possible for advertisers to broadcast their commercial messages to the nation, while regional and local radio stations could be used to promote local businesses, not unlike local newspapers.

Combined with the additional benefits that radio was free and it was an aural rather than printed medium, advertising agencies and their clients began to make heavy use of radio.

Radio programming supported by advertisers included comedy, adventure, variety, news, sports and perhaps most famously, "soap operas" – live dramatic radio shows literally sponsored by soap companies. In 1930, 12 million Americans owned a radio; by 1939, that number had more than doubled to over 28 million. During the decade, 82 out of 100 Americans listened to radio; the medium grew so popular that the 1930s later was known as the "Golden Age of Radio." Radio also became extremely important globally in communicating news and public service information once World War II began.

Depression-era retailing brought with it some lasting innovations. While small grocers were already in existence, the concept of the "supermarket" is widely believed to have been invented in 1930 by Michael J. Cullen. A former manager for Kroger Grocery & Bakery Co., Cullen conceived of a super-sized market where everything could be purchased under one roof at low prices. Stores could be located outside of cities, where real estate was cheaper.

The supermarket concept dovetailed perfectly with the increase in the number of automobiles in use by American families. Cullen called his new market "King Kullen, the world's greatest price wrecker." The supermarket had great appeal to price-conscious consumers, and a whole new way of grocery shopping was born. By 1939, the U.S. was home to more than five thousand supermarkets. Convenience was paramount, as was the interest in such mass-produced foods as canned and frozen goods. And there was never a problem parking in the expansive lots surrounding these retail behemoths.

The rise of supermarkets meant more brands were needed to stock the shelves – so the most notable brands of the decade were in the consumer packaged goods (CPG) category. Here are a number of American brands that were first introduced in the 1930s, some of which will be covered in further detail in Part II:

Alka-Seltzer
Bisquick
Chex cereal
Friskies
Fritos
Hawaiian Punch
Jiffy baking mixes
Kahlua
Kodachrome film
Kool cigarettes
Lays potato chips
Lestoil
Miracle Whip
Nescafé
Old Spice
Ritz crackers
Scotch tape
Skippy peanut butter
Snickers

SPAM
Tampax
Titleist golf balls
Tums
Twinkies
V8
View-Master
Windex

• PART II •

The American Brand and World War II

• CHAPTER 5 •

At War: Advertising and the U.S. Government

Most Americans, whatever their age, have the date December 7, 1941 burned into their memories. It marks the day that Japanese forces bombed American forces in Pearl Harbor, leading the United States to enter World War II.

Right before the onset of war, American advertising was also under attack from consumer activists and federal legislators. The advertising industry was being scrutinized because it was largely unregulated; it was also associated with and sometimes blamed for unchecked material consumption which, some believed, helped fuel the Depression.

A bill commonly known as the "Tugwell bill" (after Assistant Secretary of Agriculture Rexford Tugwell) was introduced in

June 1933 to improve food labeling laws and mandatory grading of consumer goods. A provision of the bill would have enabled the Food and Drug Administration (FDA) to broadly address false advertising. Members of the advertising community were concerned that such a bill would be too restrictive, so the advertising industry waged its own war against the bill, and a legislative battle ensued for five years. The industry relentlessly pressed its position in the media and made its case directly to the public, and the bill was ultimately unsuccessful. In its place, a considerably weaker "Wheeler-Lea Amendment" to the Federal Trade Commission Act was passed in 1938. It defined "false advertising" as follows:

> "An advertisement, other than labeling, which is misleading in a material respect; and in determining whether any advertisement is misleading, there shall be taken into account (among other things) not only representations made or suggested by statement, word, design, device, sound, or any combination thereof, but also the extent to which the advertisement fails to reveal facts material in the light of such representations or material with respect to consequences which may result from the use of the commodity to which the advertisement relates under the conditions prescribed in said advertisement, or under such conditions as are customary or usual."

In a 1939 paper for the legal journal, *Law and Contemporary Problems*, eminent attorney and legal scholar Milton Handler concluded:

"While the Wheeler-Lea Act represents a sincere attempt to stem the avalanche of false and misleading advertising, it is no more than a first, and unfortunately, inadequate step in that direction. Unless buttressed by clarifying amendments broadening its prohibitions and implementing it with effective sanctions, it will not effect an abiding solution of the vexing problem of false and misleading advertising."

Handler's conclusion represented the prevailing wisdom that the advertising industry had dodged a regulatory bullet. The late 1930s therefore appeared to be a defining moment for American advertising. However, as academician Inger Stole points out in her book, *Advertising at War*, "Advertising was still a political issue at the end of the 1930s... It was the war experience, every bit as much as the legislative battles of the 1930s, that defined the role of advertising in both our postwar political economy and our cultural firmament."

In fact, advertising became a very effective weapon during World War II, setting the stage for brand marketing to thrive in subsequent decades.

Even after the Wheeler-Lea Amendment was implemented, representatives from the advertising industry and federal regulators continued their discussions about the nature of advertising's role in the American economy.

One potentially contentious battle between the two sides was the issue of taxation. As war broke out in Europe, America amped up its defense spending even though it was not officially at war until the attack on Pearl Harbor. Congress reacted by passing a bill that taxed businesses on "excess profits" for defense but it was flawed: The bill overlooked the fact that businesses could evade the tax by simply spending more on advertising and claiming it as a business expense. An "Advertising Tax Bill" was quickly drawn up to put a stop to the practice. Once again, the advertising industry aggressively fought against the new bill and won; a subsequent bill designed to tax advertising directly also failed. As it turned out, advertising was deemed a legitimate business deduction.

Brand Advertising and the War

Despite these industry victories, the question over whether advertising was advisable at a time of conflict was not put to rest until the United States entered the war. Luckily for the advertising industry, history repeated itself – as in the Great War, the federal government again sought the assistance of advertising experts to help support the war effort.

Interestingly, it was a mere few weeks before Pearl Harbor that advertising executives met and decided to form an "Advertising Council," the purpose of which was to "bring the entire advertising industry together in service of social good," according to the website of the modern-day Ad Council, which is still in existence. But as war was declared, the concept quickly morphed into a "War Advertising Council." The timing was prophetic: The advertising industry was now able to position its own "brand" as helping in the war effort, and the federal government was only too happy to accept the industry's assistance.

The War Advertising Council (WAC) set out on a course parallel to the Committee on Public Information (CPI), the agency that was operated by the federal government during the Great War. It was similar to the CPI with one major distinction: While the CPI was formed by the Wilson Administration and reported to the president himself, the WAC was a private organization operated by the advertising industry. As such, it maintained its separation from the government and instead played a vital role in public relations, building the brand image of the advertising industry as a whole.

The WAC was not completely independent, however; it had to closely coordinate its efforts with the federal bureaucracy through such agencies as the Office of War Information, the Advertising Division of the Bureau of Campaigns and the Office of Facts and Figures. Still, the federal government not only had access to the creative and media talents of the country's leading advertising agencies, the WAC provided its services to the government at no charge – another crafty public relations move. The advertising industry could legitimately claim it was making its own considerable investment in promoting the war.

The WAC was essentially a clearinghouse for industry efforts in support of America's role in World War II, as was the CPI during the Great War. One of the Council's earliest government "clients" was none other than Henry Morgenthau Jr., the Secretary of the Treasury. Morgenthau found the WAC's assistance in promoting war bonds invaluable – so vital, in fact, that it seemed to finally put to rest any leftover concern about advertising taxation.

Eventually, the Bureau of Campaigns and the WAC became a well-oiled team, with promotional needs from all parts of the federal government flowing through the Bureau, and the WAC developing and executing projects as required. In excess of four hundred advertising agencies volunteered their services to the WAC and advertisers paid for campaigns, which invariably promoted government programs as well as an advertiser's company or brand name.

Not unlike during the Great War, advertising on behalf of America's involvement in World War II could be viewed as both patriotic and propagandistic. However, the majority of Americans were pro-war and embraced wartime advertising messages. Government agencies, along with the WAC, used every medium available, including newspapers, magazines, radio and posters for thematic advertising, as indicated below. Comic books and cartoon animation played an important pro-war role. Hollywood studios contributed by producing thinly veiled propaganda movies that glorified America and vilified its enemies. Also on the propaganda side, millions of leaflets were produced by the government and dropped by airplanes, often behind enemy lines, in an effort to convince foreign populations and sometimes even enemy soldiers to support the Allies.

The World War II Brand

World War II itself was a "megabrand" of sorts with various essential sub-brands – major war-related subject categories that received special attention. These sub-brands included:

- **Building Morale**
  It was essential to build morale on the home front as well as on the battlefield. A common dual theme – patriotism and promise – pervaded morale-building promotions. While the American people were already largely patriotic, it never hurt to remind them of the greatness of the United States and the risk of enemy victory. Patriotism was also strongly reinforced in advertising directed at American forces to remind them what they were fighting for.

  As for "promise," the word implied victory for the Allies as well as projecting a prosperous life after winning the war. Arguably, one campaign attracted the most attention when it envisioned a "Kitchen of Tomorrow," even before the war ended.

  H. Creston Doner, an industrial designer, created a fanciful sample kitchen for the Libbey-Owens-Ford Glass Company of Toledo, Ohio, and the company built a prototype experimental kitchen from his design. It appealed to the aspirations of American women (including Doner's wife, who inspired his work), teasing them with the potential modernistic convenience that would come after a victory in the war. Featured in the August 9, 1943 issue of *LIFE*, one of the most popular American magazines of the time, the kitchen was described this way:

> "All the equipment needed for preparing, cooking, storing food is built in, runs by electricity. The cabinets have sliding doors. Bending and stooping are reduced to a minimum because counters and utensils are at proper working level. Generous use of glass enables the housewife to see through the oven door and cook pots, into icebox and cupboards. Fronts of counters and drawers beneath working surfaces are slanted in so that housewife has knee room when she sits at her work. When work is done, the kitchen doubles as a playroom."

The Kitchen of Tomorrow was a big hit with consumers who wanted to dream of what postwar life would be like. Magazines and newspapers featured it, Paramount made a short film about it, and three models of the Kitchen of Tomorrow toured the country, attracting over 1-1/2 million visitors.

- **Conservation and Rationing**
  Conservation of vital resources and rationing of scarce materials, such as gasoline, nylon and rubber, were vital to the war effort. One of every seven war posters promoted the need for conservation. This was an area in which major manufacturers of products could boast

about their support of the war as well as encourage the American public to make necessary sacrifices.

Brands were not very subtle in promoting conservation; in fact, many of the appeals were emotional. For example, the tire manufacturer Goodyear depicted a mom whose son was killed in action while appealing to moms' duty with advertising copy that read in part: "You can only fall in line with friend and neighbor and, through scrap drives and conservation campaigns, play your part as fully as you can, as every good soldier on the home front should. You can only remember that every helpful act, no matter how small, not only hastens Victory but does its share to bring more boys back before their blue stars turn to gold." (Gold stars were indicative of soldiers killed in action.)

Other brands were more pragmatic; General Mills, for example, produced a Betty Crocker "cookbooklet" featuring wartime recipes incorporating the conservation/rationing message. In terms of brand impact, Lucky Strike may have been one of the more creative examples of conservation. The cigarette brand, whose name appeared in a bold red circle on the pack, changed the dark green background color to white; brand owner American Tobacco Company touted it with a slogan that became very familiar to radio listeners: "Lucky Strike Green has gone to war!" The company claimed the modification was made because the green color had to be used by the military for camouflage – but industry insiders believed the change was made to liven up the look of the brand and make it more appealing to women.

- **Farms, Nutrition and "Victory Gardens"**
America's farms needed to keep producing dairy products, meat and vegetables/fruits for both consumers and America's warriors, so maintaining farms and farm production were key messages. Related to farm maintenance, good nutrition was an important theme, along with messages promoting "Victory Gardens." These gardens became a very popular way in which consumers with a little bit of spare land could contribute to the war effort by planting vegetables.

When it came to nutrition, food companies were uniquely positioned to promote their brands as well as good nutrition. A dairy brand, the Borden Company, enlisted its renowned cartoon character cow, Elsie, as a kind of spokesperson for the National Nutrition Program. One lengthy ad that explained the program using both copy and illustrations closed with the following statement: "Elsie says: 'We at the Borden Company are so enthusiastic about the National Nutrition Program that we're using this space to tell you about it, instead of talking about our new products.'"

Victory Gardens, which actually started on the home front during the Great War, increased in popularity in World War II because of food rationing. Since the bulk of processed foods were being shipped overseas to the nation's armed forces, Americans enthusiastically embraced the grow-it-yourself philosophy. The Victory Garden was as much symbolic as it was practical, and it provided an opportunity for such brands as Birds Eye and Green Giant to promote their brand names. Green Giant, for instance, offered a free booklet entitled "The Green Giant's Secrets in Growing Peas and Corn." Some companies handed out "Victory Seeds" to consumers with product purchase – but consumers weren't always aware that these same companies received government tax breaks for their war promotion.

Victory Gardens became one of the most successful war-themed campaigns, second only to war bonds. By 1943, some twenty million Victory Gardens had been cultivated, producing close to eight million tons of vegetables and accounting for over 40 percent of the country's vegetable production.

- **Protecting War Information**
There was considerable concern about confidential information being unwittingly shared with the enemy since spies were suspected of infiltrating the United States. The War Advertising Council conceived of the legendary phrase, "Loose Lips Sink Ships," which was part of a major poster and advertising campaign.

Again, brands found ways to incorporate the notion of protecting war information into clever promotions. In one magazine ad, Smith Bros. Cough Drops (*Appendix, 5*) advised, "KEEP YOUR MOUTH SHUT! DON'T GOSSIP – it spreads rumors! DON'T COUGH – it spreads germs!" One of the best examples of this approach was advertising placed in magazines by the hatmaker, John B. Stetson Company (*Appendix, 6*). In a series of ads, the company replaced the well-worn phrase, "Keep it under your hat" with "KEEP IT UNDER YOUR STETSON." What better way to spread an important war message than in connection with a memorable and uniquely applicable promotional tagline.

- **War Bonds**
War bonds garnered the most advertising support of any other sub-brand. They were considered to be a key mechanism for raising money from private citizens to help fund America's role in the war. War bonds were easy to purchase – they were sold at post offices, banks and even at retail locations. Employees of companies could elect a payroll deduction to pay for them. War bonds became even more popular because they were not just investments in the war effort, they also generated interest paid by the U.S. government after twelve months.

Hundreds of ads encouraging consumers to buy war bonds appeared in magazines and newspapers; most of them were sponsored by advertisers who wanted to associate their brands with war bonds. War bond posters were seen everywhere and radio commercials proliferated. There was even a war bond recording made in 1942 featuring Tommy Dorsey's Orchestra and Frank Sinatra called "Dig Down Deep."

Ads ran the gamut: Some were purely informational, some played on patriotism and others tugged at the heart strings. There were so many war bond ads that the War Advertising Council had to classify them by type:

"All Out" – Ads that were 100 percent devoted to a government message with no corporate or product promotion other than the sponsoring company's name.
"Double Barreled" – Ads that emphasized a government message and also promoted a company or product separately, almost as a sidebar.
"Sneak Punch" – Ads that incorporated war themes into company or product promotions, usually in an integrated and sometimes clever way.
"Plug in a Slug" – Ads that concentrated on the company or product but added a small highlighted area to promote primarily war bonds; typically it was brief copy in a small box.
"Business as Usual" – Ads that used the war to enhance the company or product but did not make any direct appeal for war bonds or include other war themes.

Some companies went to great lengths to support the sale of war bonds. For example, the Timken Roller Bearing Company increased its corporate brand awareness by launching a series of fourteen full color, full-page magazine ads that ran for two years. Each ad featured a large illustrated portrait of a different military leader, such as General Eisenhower and Admiral Nimitz. The theme centered around supporting the military with the purchase of war bonds and the ad copy was typically very short.

- **Women at War**
  With America's young men largely going off to fight in the war, women took responsibility for working in America's factories and playing a support role in the Red Cross. In addition, some women directly engaged in the war effort by joining the military: Army - WACs (Women's Army Corps), Navy - WAVES (Women Accepted for Volunteer Emergency Service), Air Force - WASPs (Women Airforce Service Pilots) , Marine Corps - Women Reservists and Coast Guard - SPARs ("Semper Paratus, Always Ready").

Despite the essential role of women in the war, they were still viewed primarily as homemakers and subservient to men by American society in the 1940s. Much of the advertising featuring the women-at-war theme reflected this reality. For example, a full-page magazine ad run by cosmetic/perfume company Coty (*Appendix, 7*) displayed an illustration of a woman's face, beautifully made up, with a head shawl and accompanied by a gloved hand. She is peering at a man's face in shadow; he is wearing a military cap. There is nothing more in the way of copy than this headline in script type: "His duty to serve – Hers to inspire – Coty."

Not all messages portrayed women as secondary to men, however. Certainly one of the more "riveting" images of women-at-war messaging was a campaign that became known as "Rosie the Riveter" after a song with that title was released in 1942. Rosie was a fictitious character created to promote the fact that women were needed to work in manufacturing plants during the war. Believed to be based on a real worker at a munitions factory, Rosie was depicted as a strong, confident woman wearing a red and white bandana and pulling up her sleeve to show a muscle. The poster with Rosie's image and the slogan, "We Can Do It!" was originally only displayed on factory floors. However, a multimedia campaign featuring Rosie took the nation by storm, and women joined the workforce in droves. In 1943, for example, the U.S. aircraft industry had over 300,000 women employees – 65 percent of the industry's total workforce vs. one percent before the war. Rosie was an iconic representation of an American woman helping the war effort. As such, she truly represented everything a great brand should be.

The body of work produced by the War Advertising Council in association with the federal government was nothing short of remarkable in its impact. By the end of the war, advertising had directly contributed to the American war effort in the following ways:

- Conservation: 800 million pounds of tin, 538 million pounds of waste fats and 23 million tons of paper were salvaged
- Farming and nutrition: 50 million Victory Gardens were planted
- War bonds: $800 million of war bonds were issued.

Government agencies relied heavily on the War Advertising Council to produce effective, timely work. It's estimated that the advertising industry as a whole contributed something on the order of $800 million in advertising space, time and talent before the end of the war. When key members of the federal government realized the importance of the WAC's role in promoting all aspects of America's role in the war, they came to see the advertising industry as an ally instead of an adversary.

• CHAPTER 6 •

World War Brands

Brand marketers learned a powerful lesson from the Great War: Brands that advertised during the war maintained their visibility and fared better once the war ended than those who had cut their advertising budgets. World War II advertisers therefore believed that, at the end of the war, those brands that were popular before the war would be in demand again. As a result, major corporations generally agreed that promoting their brands during wartime was a wise investment.

The war itself offered brands the enviable position of being associated with a popular, patriotic historic event pitting good against evil. Sometimes referred to in marketing as "the halo effect," this meant that a brand could bask in a positive public image generated in this case by supporting the war effort. A company promoting their product could potentially be seen as a "good corporate soldier," further endearing the brand to the American consumer. Burnishing the brand perception could have real implications, ultimately helping the company increase sales of the branded product during and after the war. It was definitely a win-win for brand marketers.

Some marketers were more nimble at promoting their brands in association with the war, while other brand marketers virtually ignored the war but continued to advertise. Regardless, the savvy marketers who kept their brands visible during the war ultimately benefited.

Here are several stories about some of the American brands that were prominent during World War II – with a special emphasis on those brands that continued to promote themselves during wartime.

Select Brand Categories

Automobile, Tire and Gasoline Brands

The American automobile had already infiltrated the majority of American families by the time war was declared by the United States. In 1942, nearly 60 percent of all U.S. families owned one automobile – and some households boasted more than one. During the war, however, American auto manufacturers stopped producing civilian cars and instead turned their attention to building aircraft, engines, tanks, military vehicles and the like.

General Motors (GM), at the time the largest corporation in the world, became the largest military contractor in the world by the end of the war, responsible for $12 billion of war production. GM produced aircraft and diesel engines, canons, tanks, artillery shells/casings and countless other items, including "ducks," amphibious trucks that became essential to troops invading land from the sea. Other automobile manufacturers did their part as well: Chrysler built tanks and also helped make the atomic bomb, Ford built bomber planes, and GM brands Cadillac, Oldsmobile and Pontiac produced tanks, artillery rounds and anti-aircraft guns.

Similarly, American tire companies concentrated on manufacturing tires for military use, and American oil companies reallocated gasoline from the consumer market to be used in the war. Rubber and gasoline became precious commodities subject to rationing.

Cars, tires and gasoline may have been difficult for consumers to come by, but companies that made these products continued to advertise during the war years in an effort to show their support of the war as well as maintain brand awareness.

Cadillac, (*Appendix, 8*) for example, prominently featured its name and brand seal in extravagantly illustrated full color ads that depicted the engines, tanks and airplanes built in its factories. One such ad highlighted fighter planes above the headline, "We've put 44 million man-hours in the air!" Another ad with an illustration of a tank carried the headline, "Peacetime Power with a Wartime Job!" Both of these ads included a small box in the lower right-hand corner with copy that read, "LET'S BACK THE ATTACK BUY WAR BONDS."

General Tire was much more subtle in its approach. One of its magazine ads featured an illustration of a male soldier flirting with a pretty blond in a pink dress along with the caption, "...some things never change." The ad's headline, "For 30 years,

Generals have always been *Worth the Extra Price*," precedes copy that boasts about the quality of the tires. Only in one sentence does the ad copy mention the war: "The tire crisis is *still acute*, of course, and you must *conserve* the tires you have." But it does carry the words "BUY MORE WAR BONDS" next to an illustration of a tire.

The oil company, Texas Company (also known as Texaco), (*Appendix*, 9) ran an ad with an illustration of a Japanese and a German flag in a trash barrel, accompanied by the headline "**when?**" It read in part:

"When... will the thundering battlefields suddenly become silent? ...

It depends on **you**. Fighting will win the war...but no army can win a total war without total support from the folks back home.

You can help by buying war stamps and bonds...by conserving food...and gasoline...and rubber."

Beauty Brands
You might think when women started working in factories that they were less concerned with their appearance. Not so. In the 1940s, a woman typically wore makeup when she went out of her home. She wanted and needed to look "put together" all the time. Even the factory worker "Rosie the Riveter," mentioned earlier, was shown on a poster wearing false eyelashes, eye makeup, face powder and lipstick!

The government encouraged women to continue their beauty regimen because doing so represented a society that was not being disrupted by war. Keeping up appearances was also valuable because it was believed a pretty girl in makeup could boost a soldier's morale. Not surprisingly, pinups of girls wearing makeup, coiffed hair and bathing suits were highly prized by military men.

Some makeup ingredients were hard to come by, but that didn't stop women from being inventive – they would use beetroot in place of lipstick if necessary! A woman's makeup was such an important part of daily life that cosmetic maker Elizabeth Arden was asked to create a shade of lipstick that matched the red piping on women's military uniforms. Military women were actually issued an official kit that included nail polish, cream blush and the new "Montezuma Red" lipstick. The lipstick color was so popular that it was marketed as "Victory Red" to American female consumers.

Beauty product manufacturers advertised their brands accordingly. For example, a full-page, full color magazine ad for Ivory showed an illustration of a smiling woman in a military cap below the headline, "Keep your BEAUTY on duty!" The sub-head read, "Give your skin Ivory care, Doctors advise!"

A magazine ad for Palmolive soap depicted a woman's somewhat sad-looking face. She is holding a handwritten note from "Jim," a soldier whose photo appears in a frame in the background. His letter reads in part, "I can almost feel your soft smooth cheek against mine." The headline exclaims "Just for him – GUARD YOUR LOVELINESS! USE THE <u>ONE</u> LEADING BEAUTY SOAP... MADE WITH OLIVE AND PALM OILS!"

A Max Factor ad took a different approach, leveraging one of Hollywood's glamorous women: The ad featured the headline "Rosalind Russell in RKO-Radio's 'FLIGHT FOR FREEDOM'" along with a photo of the actress. A sub-head read, "Make up in a few seconds...look lovely for hours" with accompanying descriptive copy. The brand name was included at the bottom of the ad: "PAN-CAKE MAKE-UP Originated by Max Factor – Hollywood."

Beer Brands

The United States left Prohibition in the rear-view mirror in the 1930s and beer revived production in the United States in earnest. American beer could not have had a better ally than the federal government, which mandated that 15 percent of the beer produced in the United States had to be allocated to the armed forces during World War II. Beer was easy to transport too – canned beer had just come on the market in 1935. This gave an undisputed edge to beer as the alcoholic beverage of choice since whiskey distilleries were appropriated by the government to produce industrial alcohol.

It is not without irony that American beer was modeled after lager created in Germany. In the 1940s, American beer production was dominated by big breweries such as Anheuser Busch and the Joseph Schlitz Brewing Company (both started by German immigrants). Popular beer brands like Anheuser Busch's Budweiser and Schlitz advertised during the war, but the most effective wartime advertising in the category was actually produced by the Brewery Industry Foundation (BIF).

WORLD WAR BRANDS

The BIF highlighted two aspects of beer that resonated with wartime American consumers: Health and Patriotism.

The health claim, which was almost preposterous, suggested that brewers' yeast, actually a byproduct of brewing, could beef up soldiers' immune systems and improve workers' productivity on the home front because the yeast was an inexpensive and rich source of vitamin B complex. The specious argument was not only convincing to consumers, it succeeded in helping to obtain essential wartime industry status for breweries.

As for patriotism, the BIF (*Appendix 10*) published several ads that made it seem like beer was an integral part of the American dream and essential to building morale. The ad series carried the common headline, "MORALE IS A LOT OF LITTLE THINGS." Each ad depicted a different scene, either at home or at war. One of the ads, for example, showed an illustration of a workman apparently out in the field somewhere. He is leaning on his bed, reading a letter and smiling. The copy read in part:

"There's Bill, reading *that letter* again.

... Just a letter from the folks. Nothing very important – except to Bill.

But it's important to him all right – the way a lot of little things are to all of us.

... Little things – but they mean a lot. They chase the blues away...they help to keep *morale* up!

It happens that millions of Americans attach a special value to their right to enjoy a refreshing glass of beer...in the company of good friends...with wholesome American food...as a beverage of moderation after a good day's work.

A small thing, surely—not of crucial importance to any of us. And yet—morale *is* a lot of little things like this. Little things that help to lift the spirits, keep up the courage.

And, after all, aren't they among the things we fight for?"

Men and women in the service loved having access to an inexpensive and refreshing alcoholic beverage, and consumers believed the association between beer and America's war effort was authentic. The brand perception has endured – a staple at baseball parks, beer is seen as a patriotic beverage to this day...as American as apple pie.

Cigarette Brands
Decades before the Surgeon General of the United States declared cigarettes unhealthy, smoking was a national pastime. Its popularity during World War II increased, both on the home front and on the battlefield. In fact, the federal government required that 30 percent of all American cigarettes be allocated to the armed forces. The phrase "Smoke 'em if you got 'em" became synonymous with the military break. Miniature packs of several cigarette brands – Camel, Chesterfield, Lucky Strike and Old Gold – were part of the rations issued to the troops. Even the USO distributed cigarettes.

Comic strips and movies depicted soldiers smoking, and cigarettes were ubiquitous in war photographs. General Eisenhower was a chain smoker and President Roosevelt was frequently seen with a cigarette holder in his hand. Roosevelt even declared the tobacco leaf an essential wartime product.

It isn't surprising, then, that cigarettes played a leading role in wartime brand advertising. As mentioned earlier, Lucky Strike achieved prominence for its clever tie-in with conservation, but other cigarette brands were aggressive advertisers as well – none more than Camel. (*Appendix, 11*) Camel was distributed to soldiers more than any other cigarette brand. It didn't hesitate to boast about its supposed calming effect on soldiers in ads that targeted both American consumers and soldiers themselves. Camel ran full-page magazine advertisements to that effect, encouraging soldiers to smoke and consumers to send cigarettes to their fighting men. One ad, for example, showed an illustration of two soldiers egging on another soldier with the headline, "Attaboy, Joe... light up a Camel and look natural!" Camel even managed to draw a direct connection between soldiers and the home front: Another ad featured a military man giving a cigarette to a farmer, who exclaims, "You bet I'll have a CAMEL. They're first on the farm front, too!"

Cigarette brands had a bit of a war of their own going on at the time. When Camel claimed in an ad to be the "favorite" of Army, Navy, Marines and Coast Guard men, Chesterfield tried to one-up the brand by appealing to women. The brand ran an ad showing a woman military pilot and the headline, "With Us It's Chesterfield."

Railroad Brands

In the 1940s, America's railroads were the primary means of long-distance travel. Numerous railroad lines used advertising to promote their mode of transportation in association with the war effort. While messaging varied from line to line, it would often mention if not focus on the overall efficiency of railroads and their importance in moving both passengers and freight – especially troops and military equipment. Railroads also wanted consumers to be aware that trains might be facing delays or a reduction in amenities during the war years.

One of the train-related brand names that appeared most frequently in ads was Pullman, the company that provided trains with sleeper cars. Pullman placed close to fifty different magazine ads, most of which focused on how train travelers could help maintain railroad efficiency. For example, a 1943 ad showed an illustration of several Marines in a barracks, one of whom is holding up a photo of a girl, with this headline in quotations, "Bet I come back hitched!" The copy read in part:

"So Pullman has *another* passenger tonight – this lieutenant heading home – *another* reason wartime travel is at an all-time high. And besides the huge load on *regular* trains, an average of almost 30,000 troops a night ride *special* trains of sleeping cars.

So sometimes, it's a pretty tight squeeze to take care of *everyone*, especially in the customary Pullman manner. But most passengers realize the difficulties and are tolerant of shortcomings."

One 1942 railroad ad achieved mythic awareness for The New York, New Haven & Hartford Railroad Company, better known as The New Haven Railroad. The ad's headline, "The Kid in Upper 4," appeared above an illustration of a young soldier lying awake in the upper berth of a sleeper car as two of his buddies sleep in the lower berth. The accompanying copy is emotional and evocative. It read in part:

"It is 3:42 a.m. on a troop train. ...

One is wide awake...listening...staring into the blackness.

It is the kid in Upper 4.

Tonight, he knows, he is leaving behind a lot of little things – and big ones. ...

Next time you are on the train, remember the kid in Upper 4. ...

If there is no berth for you – it is so he may sleep.

If you have to wait for a seat in the diner – it is so he...and thousands like him...may have a meal they won't forget in the days to come.

For to treat him as our most honored guest is the least we can do to pay a mighty debt of gratitude."

Intended as a kind of apology for less than satisfactory train service, this ad was so popular that the railroad line quickly scheduled it to run in more magazines and newspapers. By early 1943, "The Kid in Upper 4" was dramatized by a radio station, it had inspired a song, MGM started production on a related film short, and more than 50,000 reprints of the ad had to be ordered to fulfill requests from the general public. Even competing railroads displayed posters of the ad in their terminals. The New Haven Railroad turned the ad into a series of "The

Kid" ads, but none of them ever matched the stunning success of the original, which won numerous awards.

Telephone Brands

The telephone was ubiquitous in American life in the 1940s, and it played a vital role in World War II. At the time, telephone service was provided nationally by "the Bell System," a collection of regional telephone operations owned by American Telephone & Telegraph (AT&T). Bell Labs was the research and development facility for AT&T. The manufacturing arm of AT&T, Western Electric, provided all of the telecommunications equipment to the Bell System. Consumers were most likely to recognize "Bell" as their brand of telephone, while businesses might be familiar with "Western Electric" as a brand name.

In 1934, the Communications Act was passed by Congress, leading to the creation of the Federal Communications Commission (FCC). Since AT&T was a monopoly, it quickly became the subject of an investigation by the FCC that resulted in the 1938-39 "Walker Report," named after Commissioner Paul Walker, which was very critical of the Bell System and Western Electric. This set the tone for future ongoing conflict between the federal government and AT&T, but any friction was put aside during World War II. The fact is Bell and Western Electric were crucial to the American war effort, even though Bell was hampered by the loss of about 70,000 employees who joined the armed services.

In wartime, Bell Labs and Western Electric shifted their focus almost entirely away from the civilian telephone market to turn their attention to military usage. Western Electric got its first order from the federal government for in excess of $700,000 worth of Signal Corps test sets as early as 1939. This was followed by telecommunications equipment for the network of military camps and bases built during the war, as well as the development and production of all sorts of electronics devices for military use, perhaps most notably radar equipment; in fact, Western Electric accounted for half of all the radar systems purchased by the U.S.

By the end of 1941, Western Electric had supplied $3.5 million worth of equipment to the federal government, a figure dwarfed by the $2.3 billion worth of equipment it provided from 1942 to 1945. After the war, Western Electric remained a government supplier to defense and space programs.

It only made sense to bolster the Bell and Western Electric brand images during wartime, so AT&T invested heavily in advertising. Western Electric (*Appendix*, 12) placed extravagantly illustrated institutional ads, often in full color. One such ad, a full page in the oversized *LIFE* magazine, depicted military communications personnel at the forefront of a huge battlefield with the headline, "COMMUNICATIONS... directing arm of combat." The accompanying text read in part: "In modern battle, our fighting units may be many miles apart. Yet every unit, every movement, is closely knit into the whole scheme of combat – through communications. Today much of this equipment is made by Western Electric, for 60 years manufacturer for the Bell System." On the battlefield were seven numbered areas representing the use of communications; for example:

"**2** Air commander radios his squadron to bomb enemy beyond river."

The extensive use of advertising by the Bell System (*Appendix, 13*) was quite different – it spoke directly to the consumer about such issues as interruptions in telephone service and reducing the use of long distance so that armed forces personnel could make calls. For instance, one ad showed a large photograph of a soldier's boots with the headline, "Put yourself in his shoes tonight." The brief accompanying copy read:

"Think how eager you'd be to talk to the folks at home if *you* were in the army and away at camp.

That's something to remember when you're thinking about making a Long Distance call between 7 and 10 o'clock at night.

You see, that's about the only time a soldier can get to the telephone. If the circuits are crowded, he may not be able to reach home before taps."

The Bell System also conceived of a little cartoon character whose torso and arms were made from a telephone. He appeared in numerous ads, reminding consumers about long distance calling and highlighting other service issues. Just as Elsie the Cow represented the Borden brand, the illustrated "telephone man" represented the Bell brand.

Individual Brands

Bob Hope

Why is a celebrity headlining a list of World War II brands? This particular celebrity – Bob Hope – was so closely associated with the war effort and so beloved that he embodies the very definition of "brand." Hope's career as a comedian and radio/film star conveniently intersected with the war. A British American, Hope at the age of four immigrated to the United States with his family. He became an American citizen in 1920. Hope held a variety of positions unrelated to entertainment but started his show business career with a vaudeville act before becoming a radio host in 1934. He began making feature films in 1938, perfectly timed for him to become a wartime personality. Hope's series of "Road" comedy films, co-starring Bing Crosby, contributed to his superstar status. Later, he became a television star as well.

Hope appeared in shows sponsored by the USO from 1941 through the war's end and beyond – until 1991, in fact. When it came to armed forces audiences, Bob Hope was both a performer and an inspiration. He loved performing in front of military crowds at home and abroad. He toured extensively, encouraging other performers to join him. During World War II, Hope starred in 144 radio broadcasts of "The Pepsodent Show;" all but nine of them were performed live in front of soldiers. About his beloved troops, he quipped that they comprised "an audience so ready for laughter, it would make what we did for a living seem like stealing money." As an aside, "The Pepsodent Show" was so popular during World War II that it helped revive the Pepsodent toothpaste brand, which had fallen out of favor by the late 1920s.

The occasional critic faulted Hope for not serving in the armed forces, but most everyone praised his dedicated, tireless service as an entertainer who boosted military morale. No one worked harder on behalf of America's armed forces. In 1997, Bob Hope was designated an "honorary veteran" by Congress, the only civilian ever to receive such an honor. Bob Hope was an enduring "brand name" revered by his country and the world.

Cheerios

American cereals are rightly associated with Boomer kids who grew up in the '50s and '60s – but cereal dates back to the mid-1800s. Cheerios is a true wartime cereal: It was introduced by General Mills as "Cheerioats" in 1941 with advertising that featured a cartoon character girl, "Cheeri O'Leary." The cereal's name was changed to "Cheerios" in 1945. The reason? Quaker Oats, the maker of oats and oatmeal, laid claim to the "oats" brand name in the cereal world – and General Mills didn't want to engage in an ugly legal battle.

According to General Mills, Cheerios was the first oat-based ready-to-eat cereal, and it didn't come easily: "More than 500 formulas were tested and more than 10 shapes and sizes were considered before our experts found the ideal combination." As unique as the ingredient and shape were, the way the round "O's" were produced was really special. Working for the company, physicist Lester Borchardt invented a gun-like machine that turned oat dough into puffed circles. The breakthrough in cereal technology was later applied to producing other General Mills cereals such as Trix, Kix and Cocoa Puffs.

Early ads boasted, "Cheerioats doesn't even look like any breakfast food you ever saw before. We blow it out of guns in the clever shape of little miniature doughnuts...fat and round and toasty-brown." Hmmm... sounds like a pretty apt description given that Cheerioats coincided with the start of World War II!

To compete with the likes of Kellogg's cereals, General Mills had to be a great cereal marketer, so the Cheerios brand became an innovator in cross-promotion. As early as 1941, General Mills used Cheerios in its sponsorship of the weekly Lone Ranger radio broadcast, which had twenty million listeners. This relationship continued when the Lone Ranger transitioned to television, and it lasted until the show's final episode in 1957.

During the Cheerios-Lone Ranger relationship, kids were delighted to find offers for Lone Ranger toys, masks, pocket-sized comic books and posters promoted on the familiar yellow Cheerios box. Some premiums were even inserted into the box. One of the most popular promotions was the Lone Ranger Frontier Town in 1948. Cut-outs of Frontier Town buildings were included on Cheerios boxes, and kids could mail in for additional buildings and maps.

What began as a wartime cereal has matured into a legendary brand. Television commercials of the 1950s featured the animated "Cheerios Kid," well-known to Boomer kids. The brand was promoted using such popular cartoon characters as Rocky and Bullwinkle in the 1960s. Cheerios kept up with its Boomer audience through adolescence, enjoying co-promotions with Disney's Mickey Mouse Club and becoming one of only two sponsors of Dick Clark's "American Bandstand" television show. The Cheerios product family today includes many varieties and remains a top-selling cereal brand.

Coca-Cola

Coca-Cola was already an internationally popular soft drink when the war started. Despite battling with Pepsi-Cola, the other popular cola of the time, Coca-Cola claimed its position as the original; the soft drink's slogan in 1942 was, "The Only Thing Like Coca-Cola is Coca-Cola Itself." The company aimed to cement that position by making a bold wartime offer, pledging "that every soldier in the field would be able to buy a Coke for a nickel, regardless of what it cost the company," according to Coca-Cola.

Coca-Cola made good on its promise when casual Coke drinker General Dwight D. Eisenhower in June 1943 urgently requested the company to ship materials and equipment for ten bottling plants to be built overseas. Included in the request was an order for three million filled bottles of Coca-Cola.

Here's where the story gets even better. Within six months of the request, a company engineer had flown to Algiers in northern Africa to open the first Coca-Cola plant. Not ten but sixty-four bottling plants were eventually shipped abroad during the war. The plants were located as close as possible to European and Pacific battlegrounds so soldiers would always have access to the beverage.

To operate the plants, some 150 "Technical Observers" – Coca-Cola employees – were brought in to serve Coke to every GI, wherever they happened to be located. The employees dressed in fatigues and were treated deferentially. They may not have fought in the war, but they were nicknamed "Coca-Cola Colonels" by the thankful service men and women. Coca-Cola was a welcome morale booster that continued to be served to the troops throughout the war: Five billion bottles were consumed by service personnel during World War II, not to mention the Coca-Cola served up through dispensers and on the field.

Meanwhile, on the home front, Coca-Cola continued to produce the beverage for consumers, even though sugar was being rationed. By operating an ammunition loading plant in Alabama and distributing Coke to troops for five cents a bottle, the Coca-Cola Company qualified to be excluded from sugar rationing during the war. Pepsi-Cola was popular as well, but it had to seek out sugar in Mexico for beverage production. Pepsi never could match the manner in which Coca-Cola penetrated the armed forces – or its public relations value.

While Pepsi-Cola (*Appendix, 14*) did not heavily engage in war-related advertising, Coca-Cola typically produced beautifully illustrated full-page, full color ads that frequently touted the morale of soldiers and war workers. For example, one ad suggested, "Next to wives, sweethearts and letters from home, among things our soldiers mention most is Coca-Cola."

Another ad boasted, "Simple pleasures build up morale and peace of mind. That's one reason why the enjoyment of ice-cold Coca-Cola has new meaning in wartime." Coca-Cola was always working on ways to integrate a war message into its advertising, even during the holiday season. According to the company, "One of our early Christmas ads featuring the famous Coca-Cola Santa Claus even had a war bond poking out of Santa's bag. Santa and the company were supporting the war effort."

Many of the company's war era ads referred to Coca-Cola's well-known slogan from 1929, "The Pause that Refreshes." Some ads also alluded to Coca-Cola as "The Real Thing," a phrase that would be adopted as the soft drink's slogan in the 1960s.

Disney

Just before the war, Walt Disney was coming off one of the highlights of his career. His animated feature film, *Snow White*, had been released in 1937. The next year, Disney was awarded an honorary Oscar for the film at the 1938 annual Academy Awards, but like Walt's film, the presentation was one-of-a-kind: Shirley Temple presented Walt Disney with one regular size Oscar, as well as seven miniature statuettes, one for each of the Seven Dwarfs!

There was no question that Walt Disney's cartoon characters were already loved throughout America and the world, but World War II brought his young company even greater admiration. The day after Pearl Harbor, Disney allowed the U.S. armed forces to "invade" his Burbank, California studios, making it the only Hollywood studio to ever be occupied by the military.

Half of the studio functioned as anti-aircraft protection for a nearby Lockheed aircraft plant for eight months.

Disney and his staff were almost immediately immersed in the war effort. According to the Walt Disney Family Museum, they devoted "over 90% of their wartime output to producing training, propaganda, entertainment, and public-service films, while also designing an extensive collection of insignia and print media." Naturally, the animation for which Disney Studios was so renowned became the centerpiece of training films and educational shorts, such as "Donald Gets Drafted" (1942) and "Fall Out – Fall In" (1943), both featuring Donald Duck.

During the early 1940s, Disney was prolific when it came to war propaganda, producing films for numerous divisions of the government as well as the armed forces. In "The Spirit of '43," made on behalf of the Treasury Department, Donald Duck explains the importance of income taxes to the war effort; the film was seen by 26 million Americans. Anti-German and anti-Japanese films were also produced, such as "Der Feuhrer's Face" (1943) and "Commando Duck" (1944). Both of these films starred Donald Duck, who demonstrated his patriotism in the first film while single-handedly destroying a Japanese airbase in the second film.

The talent of Disney's artists was also applied to children's war stamp books, posters, certificates of war bond purchase, food rationing books and Victory Garden contest record books, among other things. Donald Duck, Mickey Mouse and other Disney characters were prominent in a multitude of media.

Donald Duck in particular was lauded by *The New York Times* in 1943 as "a salesman of the American Way." Perhaps most unusual, Disney artists also created in excess of 1,200 specially designed combat insignia for all branches of the U.S. military – and even for Allied armed forces.

With his fervently patriotic role in World War II, Walt Disney further embedded himself into global consumer consciousness as a representative of one of the most patriotic and cherished American brands.

Duck (Duct) Tape

Duck or duct tape was a product born of a World War II mother's ingenuity. With two sons in the U.S. Navy, Vesta Stoudt was helping the war effort by working in an Illinois ordnance plant. As she packed and inspected boxes of ammunition, she was struck by the fact that the paper tape used to seal the boxes was inadequate. She came up with the idea of a waterproof cloth tape instead and, when plant supervisors ignored it, she decided to write a letter about it directly to President Franklin D. Roosevelt. He liked the idea and forwarded it to the War Production Board, where it was approved for production.

The Industrial Tape Corporation, an operating company of Johnson & Johnson that was later renamed Permacel, was tapped to make the tape. The tape was waterproof, cloth-based for strength, green and had an adhesive backing – but no name. Soldiers just called it "100-mile-per-hour tape" because they could quickly fix anything with it, whether it was a jeep fender or an Army boot.

So how did duck (or duct) tape get its name? That's where history gets a little muddled. It's believed that the word "duck" in the name refers to the original cotton duck cloth that was used to make the tape – or perhaps to the fact that the tape is water-resistant, like a duck. After the war, duck tape was manufactured in a grey color, which made it ideal for fixing air ducts; hence it became known as "duct tape."

Since "duct" tape wasn't trademarked, it became a generic term. Duct tape is currently manufactured by numerous different companies, but one company was wise enough to register the trademark for "Duck Tape" brand duct tape.

As do-it-yourselfers today will attest, whatever you want to call it, this stuff can hold just about anything together, in any weather. And that's what made "duck tape" essential in World War II.

Florida Citrus Commission
If you are one of the millions of Americans who starts the day with a glass of orange juice, you can at least in part thank the U.S. military. That's because the military played a direct, unusual role in making Florida orange juice an American breakfast staple.

During World War II, military officials were concerned that troops were getting the proper nutrition. Scurvy, caused by the lack of fruits and vegetables in a diet, had been known to have devastating effects during previous wars. Vitamin C was the key to maintaining good health and preventing scurvy, but shipping fresh fruit to battlefields around the world was problematic. Instead, the U.S. government obtained huge amounts of fruit from Florida citrus growers in another form: canned grapefruit and orange juice. Growers were only too happy to oblige, but they couldn't process the fruit fast enough. That's when the government stepped in. Some 10,000 German prisoners of war were located in Florida POW camps, and they became the labor pool for building a 65-acre processing plant that's still in use today.

Canned grapefruit juice was actually more common than canned orange juice at the time. The Florida Citrus Commission (*Appendix, 15*) promoted the patriotic efforts of their growers to consumers in a series of ads that explained why canned grapefruit juice was in short supply – because "Victory Vitamin C" was needed by the armed forces. The headline for one full color magazine ad, with an illustration of a PT boat in action, read, "Because every crew must have 'Victory Vitamin C' – maybe your canned grapefruit juice… is aboard Pearl Harbor's swift avengers!"

But it was canned orange juice that became more popular than the bitter grapefruit juice with soldiers, turning Florida into the nation's top orange producer – surpassing California for the first time. When the war ended, soldiers returning home were delighted to witness the emergence of a brand new product: frozen concentrated orange juice, which tasted fresher than the canned variety. Turns out the Florida Citrus Commission collaborated with the U.S. Department of Agriculture to develop a better method of preserving orange juice that led to its popularity with consumers. The preferred breakfast drink had arrived.

Hoover

The Hoover vacuum is one of those American success stories that's almost too good to be true. James Murray Spangler was working as a janitor in a Canton, Ohio department store. An asthma sufferer, he wanted to find a way to collect dust without having coughing fits. Since necessity is the mother of invention, Spangler conceived of an upright electric cleaner, using a sewing machine motor and ceiling fan blades, to suck up the dust into a cloth bag. He tested and refined the design, patented the cleaning machine in 1908 and formed the Electric Suction Sweeper Company to manufacture and sell it.

Spangler sold the first one to his cousin, Susan, who was married to William H. Hoover. Susan raved about it to her husband. Hoover, nicknamed "Boss," ran a leather goods business but he was intrigued with the machine. Spangler's tiny company was running out of money, so Boss Hoover invested in it, put Spangler on the payroll, and operated the new business out of his leather shop. The company's name was changed to Hoover in 1910 and the new machine was marketed with a 10-day free in-home trial – a unique offer at the time. Sales took off and Hoover quickly opened divisions in Canada in 1911 and then in England in 1919 (where vacuuming is still often called "hoovering.") That was the beginning of what was to become the largest vacuum machine manufacturer in the world.

Re-named in 1922, The Hoover Company kept its headquarters in North Canton, Ohio. During World War II, the federal government contracted with the company to produce items needed to support the war effort, including bomb fuses, electric motors and helmet liners. The Hoover Company discontinued vacuum cleaners temporarily but continued to manufacture parts for the four million vacuums already in use by U.S. housewives. Company president H. W. Hoover Sr. also helped organize the evacuation of 84 children, whose parents worked for Hoover, from England to the United States. Most of them lived with families in North Canton to stay safe while the war raged.

The Hoover Company (*Appendix, 16*) advertised during the war and after it ended. Their magazine advertising tended toward long copy that often drew a relationship between the company, its products and the war effort. One ad carried the headline, "The 'V-Home'.... Is your home one?" The text discussed what was needed to receive a sticker that could be applied to the window of a home as certification that consumers were doing their part in the war effort; for example, "People who live in V-Homes get out the scrap and turn it in…" and "V-Homes buy War Stamps and Bonds regularly…" Accompanying copy about Hoover read in part:

"The Hoover Company is working today for all American homes – not with cleaners, but in the manufacture of war materials.
The Hoover Company is glad to take this space to urge you to turn your Home Sweet Home into a Home V-Home—right now. Let's fight *with* the homes we're fighting *for*."

Before the war ended, The Hoover Company became a public company. It returned to manufacturing vacuum cleaners after the war.

Jeep

While numerous brands can lay claim to supporting the war effort, few of them played such an integral part in actual battle during the war as did Jeep, originally a slang term used by the U.S. Army to describe new recruits or vehicles. In fact, "Jeep" didn't become a brand name until 1945, when the first civilian Jeep was introduced.

The U.S. Army asked 135 automakers to bid on manufacturing a "light reconnaissance vehicle," but only three companies, Bantam, Ford and Willys (*Appendix, 17*), were interested. They worked together to come up with a design in 75 days, and in late 1940, Willys-Overland made a prototype labeled "Quad" because it boasted a 4x4 system, today referred to as 4-wheel drive. While the design was approved, the Army thought the vehicle was too heavy, so Willys created the MA, a lighter version of the Quad.

In July, 1941, before the United States even entered the war, Willys-Overland was tapped to manufacture a version of the MA that included modifications required by the military called the MB. In the meantime, MAs were provided to Allied forces until the MB could roll off the assembly line. The Willys MB became the iconic vehicle so often seen in battle and in war movies. It was an essential piece of equipment for GIs everywhere – as important as their firearms.

This forerunner of contemporary SUVs was so dependable, versatile and valuable that General George C. Marshall called it "America's greatest contribution to modern warfare." The Willys MB was the primary light wheeled transport vehicle for the United States and its allies during World War II. Approximately 650,000 of them were manufactured, making it the first mass-produced four-wheel drive vehicle. Legend has it that one damaged MB was sent home with a Purple Heart.

The utility of the war vehicle was such that, as soon as the war ended, Willys-Overland converted the MB into a "CJ," or Civilian Jeep, focusing first on the farm market. In 1945, there were some 5-1/2 million farmers in the U.S., the majority of whom didn't have trucks or tractors. The CJ could fill a real need not just on farms, but anywhere a work vehicle was warranted. The storied Jeep was a direct outgrowth of World War II. Even though other brands have attempted to trade on the Jeep's fame, appearance and utility, to this day, there is only one "Jeep" brand. It is now a much-loved contemporary car brand that's available even in luxury models.

LIFE
No magazine brand name was better known in the 1940s and 1950s than LIFE magazine. In 1936, Henry Luce, who also published TIME and FORTUNE magazines, bought the rights to the name LIFE and turned it from a weekly humor publication into a weekly newsmagazine. Over the years, the magazine itself seemed larger than life, largely because of its superb, award-winning photojournalism.

With its bold, universally recognized masthead (white capitalized letters on a red background) and oversized pages, LIFE was ideally suited to report on the war in pre-TV America. Reporters and photographers covered the war around the globe as well as on the home front and LIFE chronicled history as it happened. LIFE reached a circulation high point of over 13 million as readers stayed glued to its stories and photographs. It was also a primary vehicle for brand advertisers to place often full color, elaborately illustrated ads boasting of their support for World War II. When the war was won, brand advertisers used the pages of LIFE to reassure consumers that their products were available once again.

LIFE covered the world's most important stories, including the Vietnam War, through the early 1970s. As a weekly, it ceased publication in 1972, but continued as a series of "LIFE Special Reports" for the next six years. LIFE then transitioned to a monthly publication. By the year 2000, LIFE had run its course. Still, even the magazine's ending was momentous: The last issue featured a story entitled "A Life Ends," an account of a man named George Story who died in April 2000. That same man was featured as a baby in a story entitled "Life Begins," published in the very first issue of LIFE magazine in 1936.

M&Ms
M&Ms, the beloved American candy that "melts in your mouth, not in your hands," was an invention that coincided with World War II and became an energy-boosting food for American soldiers. Forrest Mars. Sr., the son of Frank C. Mars, who founded the Mars Company, is said to have seen soldiers in the Spanish

Civil War of the 1930s eating chocolate covered in a hard shell, which prevented the chocolate from melting. They turned out to be Smarties, a British-made confection. Mars liked the idea so much that he patented his own process and began producing a similar candy in the United States in 1941. While first intended for consumers, the outbreak of the war changed his plans.

Mars had trouble obtaining chocolate, since it was being rationed. To get access to the chocolate, he teamed up with Bruce Murrie, the son of William F. R. Murrie, who was president of Hershey's Chocolate, a competitor. The candy was christened "M&M" in their honor, and the M&Ms were quickly commandeered by the U.S. Army for its unique heat-resistant qualities. All during the war, the candy was sold exclusively to the military; in fact, tubes (not bags) of M&Ms were included in soldiers' rations. The Newark, New Jersey factory produced some 200,000 pounds of M&Ms per week. Incidentally, another hard candy the military purchased because it could withstand the rigors of battle was NECCO Wafers.

Ads for M&Ms during the war proclaimed they were "100% at War," whetting consumers' appetites for their much-anticipated post-war distribution. When the war was over, soldiers clamored for M&Ms and Mars was happy to meet the demand. M&Ms were sold to consumers in tubes, in brown, yellow, orange, red, green and violet colors, until 1948, when the packaging transitioned to bags. Since then, of course, more colors and flavor variations that stretch beyond plain chocolate have been added to the brand family – even though the familiar candy shell remains. Contests have periodically been held to select new colors and flavors. The iconic M&M animated cartoon characters seen in television commercials have taken on celebrity status.

M&Ms were an important wartime product, but the military also relied on good old chocolate bars – another reason chocolate was so hard to come by during the war. Hershey was asked to develop "U.S. Army Field Ration D," a special chocolate bar designed to provide a quick burst of energy when needed in the field, as well as a "tropical" bar that could withstand extreme temperatures. Chocolate bars were part of regular rations; they also became symbolic of victory when American soldiers would hand chocolate out to children who greeted them along the streets of villages and towns they liberated from enemy forces.

Motorola Radio
The Motorola brand name became widely known during World War II because of an innovation called the "Handie-Talkie," also sometimes referred to as a "walkie talkie." As World War II was beginning, Galvin Manufacturing Corporation (which later became Motorola Radio) recognized the need for a portable two-way radio that could be carried by soldiers. Engineer Donald Mitchell developed such a radio, but the U.S. Army Signal Corps thought its range of just one mile was inadequate. Mitchell and his team improved the technology by turning the device into a two-way AM radio that could be operated with just one hand. The 5-pound, battery operated SCR536 (informally known as the Handie-Talkie) was thought to be ideal for paratroopers, so Galvin was awarded a contract to produce them before the United States entered the war.

The radio-telephone ended up being so useful to paratroopers that the Army ordered them for infantrymen as well. Some 130,000 units were produced by the Motorola Radio division of Galvin, as well as other firms, by the end of the war. The Handie-Talkie played a key role in allowing troop leaders to communicate with field headquarters. Germans who captured a few of them were said to be very impressed with the technology.

Galvin (*Appendix, 18*) placed self-congratulatory magazine ads during the war boasting about the Handie-Talkie. One ad carried an illustration of a soldier speaking on the radio with the headline, "THE 'FIGHTINGEST' RADIO IN THE ARMED SERVICES." The ad copy read in part:

> "The men who do the fighting *like* the Motorola-built Handie-Talkie. They say without qualification…'It's fine… just like having a house telephone at your fingertips. We feel safer, stronger because we're always in touch with our command post! Yes, sir, the Handie-Talkie is the "fightingest" 2-way radio in this war!'
>
> Now and as long as there is an enemy gun pointed at an American fighter, the business of Motorola Electronics Engineers will be *Communications for Victory*."

That's how the Motorola brand got its start. Eventually, Motorola became known for televisions, cell phones and other innovative communications technology.

Nash-Kelvinator

An unusual marriage of two companies in 1937 ended up directly benefiting the American war effort. That's when Nash Motors, an automobile manufacturer, joined with Kelvinator Appliance Company, which produced consumer appliances such as refrigerators. Each brand had its own unique identity and its own customer base, but they decided to consolidate their business operations. During the war, Nash-Kelvinator (*Appendix*, 19) became an important and valued partner to the American military, producing more helicopters than any other company, including the R-6A Hoverfly II, the most advanced Sikorsky helicopter design of the war.

Nash-Kelvinator also manufactured Pratt & Whitney Aircraft engines, Hamilton Standard propellers rocket motors, bomb fuses, two-wheel cargo trailers, aviation pressure gauges and even binoculars. A planned four-engine sea plane was designed but not built.

Nash-Kelvinator's institutional advertising made sure the American public was aware that the corporation was supporting the war effort. One magazine ad showed American aircraft in flight, accompanied by the headline, "A REFRIGERATOR AND AN AUTOMOBILE GO TO WAR!" Obviously, this was a reference to the company's dual product line.

Another magazine ad played on emotions and plucked the heartstrings: The ad depicted an unsmiling woman with the headline, "'WHEN YOU COME BACK TO ME...'" The ad copy was written entirely in the first person, as if the woman was addressing her husband who is fighting in the war. It is a description of everyday life with some stirring language, such as, "We are so proud of you. Proud that you are making sure that hate and greed and tyranny will never rise to threaten us again. And we are proud to make our own sacrifices, knowing that they will help to bring you back to us sooner."

Nash-Kelvinator acquired the Hudson Motor Car Company in 1954; this led to the formation of the American Motors Corporation. In 1968, White-Westinghouse purchased the Kelvinator brand.

Nescafé

Contrary to popular belief, Nescafé, an instant coffee product made by the Swiss company Nestlé, wasn't the first instant coffee. But when Nescafé came to market in 1938, it set the standard and soon became a product enjoyed by soldiers and consumers alike.

Instant coffee was first invented way back in 1901; however, it was in 1910 that an American coincidentally named George Washington figured out how to mass produce instant coffee. He started the G. Washington Coffee Refining Co. (*Appendix*, 20) in New York and sold it to consumers. The product's popularity really hit a high point when America entered the Great War in 1917. Packaged in envelopes, the U.S. military bought as much of the powdered coffee as it could. Soldiers loved having instant hot coffee in combat, crowing about the "cup of George" they could enjoy on the front lines.

In 1938, the larger Nestlé company made an international splash with Nescafé, (*Appendix, 21*) which quickly became the dominant brand of instant coffee. This probably contributed to George Washington selling his company in 1943. The "cup of George" became a "cup of Joe," quite possibly because GIs were generically known as "GI Joes."

According to Nestlé, Nescafé was so popular with Americans during World War II – a key reason was its longer shelf life than fresh coffee – that two U.S. production facilities had to be established by 1943. The majority of the instant coffee product was supplied to U.S. troops. At the time, just three countries accounted for more than 75 percent of Nescafé's consumption: the United States, the United Kingdom and Switzerland.

Today, Nescafé remains a popular global brand.

Nucoa
Food shortages during World War II created hardships for some branded products but opportunities for others, such as Nucoa, a margarine brand. Prior to the war, butter was the accepted standard in American households and margarine was largely frowned upon. Margarine had first been invented in France in 1868, but modern margarine is generally associated with a process called hydrogenation of oils; Nucoa, introduced in 1917, was one of the first to use this process.

There was considerable condemnation of margarine in the early 1900s, thanks largely to the dairy industry, which lobbied for laws that prevented margarine from being yellow in color so it wouldn't compete with butter. It was hard to depress consumer interest in margarine, though, because the product was less than half the cost of butter.

World War I saw a boost in margarine use, but sales really boomed during World War II due to butter rationing. Vegetable oil-based "oleomargarine," as it was called, became very popular, even though laws through the 1930s in several states continued to ban its yellow color. Clever margarine manufacturers included yellow powder pellets with the white margarine so consumers could simulate the color of butter – even though doing so meant mushing the yellow powder into the oily substance by hand! Margarine was helped along by health studies in the early 1940s pointing to the benefits of vegetable oil over animal fat.

Nucoa, manufactured by Best Foods, was the top selling margarine during World War II, but other competing brands, such as Parkay by Kraft Foods (1937) and Blue Bonnet by Standard Brands (1943), expanded the market. With the popularity of margarine no longer in doubt, state laws began to change. By 1950, a federal law appropriately named the Margarine Act removed restrictions on the product.

Nucoa (*Appendix*, 22) participated in wartime advertising, emphasizing the brand's usage on the home front. One ad, for example, showed photographs of Lloyd Miller and his family – Miller was described as a "skilled worker making precision tools for Uncle Sam." The headline was supposedly a quote from Mrs. Miller, who said, "I'll say Nucoa is a Food for Defense!" The ad copy largely concentrated on the supposed health benefits of Nucoa margarine.

Nylon

The story of nylon (*Appendix, 23*) can't be covered up: It has actually been called "the fiber that won the war." Prior to 1940, women wore silk stockings. Silk, which was imported primarily from Japan, wasn't the best material for stockings because it didn't stretch, tore easily and was difficult to wash. A chemist named Wallace Hume Carothers who worked for the DuPont Company (*Appendix, 24*) solved the problem. Carothers invented a material that was stretchable, durable and washable. Dupont attempted to trademark it as "nuron" ("no run" spelled backwards), but because of a trademark conflict, DuPont changed the name to "nylon." It would become a brand name synonymous with stockings.

Right from their introduction in late 1939, nylon stockings were a big hit with women – DuPont sold out an initial test quantity of 4,000 pairs in just three hours. When the stockings were rolled out to the public on "Nylon Day" (May 16, 1940), U.S. department stores sold four million pairs of brown nylon stockings within two days. Consumer demand was supplanted by military demand when war was declared. It turned out that nylon was a highly valuable material in manufacturing a host of war-related items, from parachutes to mosquito netting to ropes and even aircraft fuel tanks.

Since the United States was at war with Japan, the supply of silk was non-existent and nylon was virtually unavailable (except at black market prices). Women had to use their ingenuity, so they adopted a new kind of "stocking" that was actually liquid makeup applied to the legs. Black eyeliner pencil was used to draw "seams" up the fake nylon backs.

With the end of the war, nylon stockings came back, and demand had built up to the extent that there were "nylon riots" across the country in 1945. Women stormed stores to purchase stockings. You might say there was quite a run on them.

Oneida
Established in 1848 in Oneida, New York, Oneida Ltd. was a leading producer of the "Community" brand of silverplate flatware. Oneida played an important role in the Great War, adapting its manufacturing plants to make ammunition clips, combat knives and surgical instruments. During World War II, Oneida manufactured those items as well as aircraft survival kits, army trucks, basic flatware and jet engine parts.

The most interesting brand aspect of Oneida's wartime story, though, was its highly successful advertising campaign. The company had ceased production of flatware during the war, but it wanted the American public to remember its Community brand while realizing that Oneida was an active participant in the war effort. A series of ads, beautifully illustrated in full color by Jon Whitcomb with the theme "Back Home for Keeps," centered around the eventual reunion of soldiers with loved ones. One such ad depicts an airman kissing his girl. The copy reads:

"**Today he has a war on his hands.** But the day will come, please God, when *your* Tom or Dick or Jack comes home for keeps... when kisses will be real, not paper; when you may know the good feel of a tweedy shoulder, the dear sound of a longed-for voice, a strong hand on yours in a dim-lit room...when crystal will gleam and silver will sparkle on a table set for two.

To that day we of Community are bending every effort to speed the work of war. On that day we pledge again to make the loveliest silverware patterns that ever graced a radiantly happy table. Are you doing a little *personal* post-war planning? So are we – at Community. *And the day will come!*"

Twenty-one of these ads ran from 1943 through 1945. The series was so popular with consumers that Oneida received half a million requests for reprints. The ads even inspired a romantic ballad. Oneida subsequently produced a similarly illustrated second series of ads with the theme, "These are the things we are fighting for."

"PB&J"

"PB&J" isn't officially a brand, but it may as well be one. The PB&J, or Peanut Butter & Jelly – that delectable sandwich kids have favored for generations – was already forty years old when it was enthusiastically embraced by U.S. servicemen. Apparently, the very first recipe for a PB&J appeared in 1901. But its rise to fame didn't happen until peanut butter became truly spreadable, grape jelly was invented and sliced white bread was ubiquitous.

Peanut butter and jelly sandwiches were a natural for World War II troops. Peanut butter was inexpensive, portable and protein-packed, jelly had already become a staple in the Great War and sliced bread was easy to use. Soldiers liked the salty-sweet taste that made for a quick, nutritious meal.

Peanut butter itself was already known as a cheap protein substitute during the Great Depression; it was just as popular with consumers during World War II because it was still inexpensive and it wasn't rationed. When soldiers came home, they returned with a hankering for PB&J – and it quickly became an American tradition, loved by soldiers and their kids alike. The classic PB&J sandwich consisted of Wonder bread smeared with Peter Pan or Skippy peanut butter topped with Welch's grape jelly.

Philco
Philco may not be a widely recognized brand name today, but you could easily consider Philco the "Apple" of the radio era. Philco was established in 1892 in Philadelphia (hence its name). In 1928, the company made a wise decision to enter the radio market; just two years later, Philco became the leading American radio brand and remained the top radio manufacturer until the 1950s.

The company was so prolific in manufacturing radios that it managed to produce nine new models in 1942, even after the United States entered the war. Like many other manufacturers, however, Philco was inspired to repurpose its manufacturing operation in support of the war effort, so it virtually halted radio production until the war's end.

But that didn't stop the company from advertising; in fact, Philco became known not just for the sheer number of its patriotic institutional ads but also for the creative approach of the advertising. A series of more than sixty black-and-white ads each featured cartoons drawn and signed by over twenty nationally recognized editorial cartoonists. The cartoons often portrayed the enemy in a derogatory but wildly funny way. One ad, for example, carried the headline "DIG 'EM OUT!" The accompanying cartoon showed the Uncle Sam character as a soldier, using a shovel with the words "WHAT IT TAKES" to dig out a rat's nest from the earth. Inside the rat's nest, Hitler (Germany) and Hirohito (Japan) are depicted as, you guessed it, rats!

Accompanying ad copy indicated that this ad, along with others in the series, was posted in Philco factories "as an inspiration to the men and women who are helping to produce the weapons of victory." At the end of this particular ad, Philco offered to send a reproduction of the original drawing by C. H. Sykes to anyone who requested it.

Raisin Bran
Cereal – the breakfast food popularized by Boomer kids – was around long before the start of World War II, as mentioned earlier. That included a cereal called "Raisin Bran." It may surprise you to learn that the first raisin bran, named Skinner's Raisin Bran and manufactured by the Uncle Sam Breakfast

Food Company, was introduced in 1926. In 1942, however, Kellogg and Post, two leading cereal makers, got into the act. They both co-opted the name "Raisin Bran," much to Skinner's dismay. A trademark infringement case ensued, but the Skinner brand lost in court. That meant any company could produce their own "raisin bran." Skinner's Raisin Bran eventually faded into obscurity while Kellogg and Post gained market share.

During the war, Kellogg's Raisin Bran was popular with consumers, even as Kellogg turned its attention to helping the U.S. armed forces by producing 43 million "K-rations," which were individually packaged daily food rations. (The "K" in K-rations bore no relation to Kellogg.) Kellogg's machine shops were also used to manufacture wartime supplies. Kellogg's wartime advertising promoted its entire cereal line as foods that were nutritional, ready-to-eat and saved time and money.

Not surprisingly, the Kellogg Company's marketing muscle subsequently turned Kellogg's Raisin Bran into the leading brand of raisin bran – and it still is today.

Ray-Ban
The first pair of Ray-Ban sunglasses was designed by Bausch & Lomb at the request of John Macready, a United States Army Air Corps colonel. He wanted glasses that would reduce glare for pilots, whose planes were able to fly higher and higher as aeronautic technology improved. The project began in 1929 and a prototype of anti-glare aviator sunglasses which could "ban" the sun's rays was developed in 1936. Glasses with plastic frames were made available to pilots and consumers in 1937; the

next year, they were redesigned in the soon-to-be-classic shape with metal frames and branded "Ray-Ban Aviator" sunglasses.

The timing couldn't have been better, because when war broke out, Ray-Ban was there. The glasses were enhanced with a gradient from dark at the top to lighter at the bottom so fighter pilots could more easily see the instrument panels of their airplanes. General Douglas MacArthur became an unwitting endorsement for Ray-Ban when photographs showed MacArthur wearing them in the Philippines.

Ray-Ban's military popularity translated into broad consumer acceptance for the brand. More models were introduced and by the 1950s, such Hollywood celebrities as James Dean wore them. The Ray-Ban brand is still part of pop culture – Tom Cruise immortalized them in the 1986 movie, "Top Gun." Aviators are the favorite sunglasses of American President Joe Biden, who was often seen wearing them outdoors. The 2020 Biden presidential campaign even used the iconic shades as a symbol on lawn signs.

RCA

The storied history of RCA (Radio Corporation of America) includes entanglements with other major American corporations, a diverse line of innovative products, and a major role in World War II. Founded in 1919, RCA was co-owned by AT&T, General Electric, United Fruit Company and Westinghouse. In 1932, however, an antitrust settlement with the U.S. Government led to RCA becoming an independent company.

RCA (*Appendix, 25*) was an early innovator in the radio industry, not only as a manufacturer of radios, but as the originator of NBC, the first national American radio broadcasting network. Later, RCA created television sets and was one of the developers of color television.

In the 1930s and 1940s, RCA was best known for both its radios and its phonographs, most notably the "Victrola," produced by the RCA Victor division. The company had acquired the Victor Talking Machine Company in 1929. RCA Victor also innovated when it came to records – the company introduced the first 33-1/3 RPM record in 1931, which was a commercial failure because of the Great Depression, and also created the first 45 RPM record in 1949. RCA Victor did not revive the 33-1/3 RPM record until 1950 in response to a competitor.

During World War II, RCA's manufacturing plants, as well as its research and development facility, RCA Laboratories, were devoted to the war effort. In 1942, the company worked on a secret project for the U.S. Navy code-named "Madame X." The outcome of the project was a device called the proximity fuse, which allowed electronic detonation of a bomb. RCA was also tapped by the military for radar and radio development. RCA's wartime advertising largely concentrated in the value of music as a morale-booster. Even after the war, RCA continued to work on government projects that included defense and space exploration.

RCA was re-acquired in 1985 by General Electric, but that didn't work out very well. RCA's various divisions and product lines were sold off over several years. Now all that remains is the RCA brand name, which still appears on some consumer electronics.

Silly Putty

Strangely enough, Silly Putty was a World War II invention that went wrong. With the country's Asian-based rubber supply in jeopardy because of Japan's entry into the war, American manufacturers wanted to come up with a synthetic rubber substitute. James Wright, a General Electric chemical engineer, created a putty-like substance made from boric acid and silicone oil in 1943 that could be stretched and bounced higher than rubber. But the material had other quirky attributes: It could slowly flow like a liquid, be broken into pieces when hit hard with a hammer, and transfer images from newspaper onto itself.

The U.S. government wasn't interested in the product, but a toy marketer named Peter Hodgson got hold of it a few years later. Hodgson came up with the name "Silly Putty" and packaged the weird stuff in plastic eggs because he wanted to sell them around Easter for one dollar each. A 1950 magazine article about Silly Putty resulted in more than 250,000 units selling in just three days. The toy became a sensation with Boomer kids and sold millions more. It wasn't just kids who liked Silly Putty – in 1968, Apollo 8 astronauts used it to secure their tools in zero gravity! Silly Putty was a fad that lasted; today the brand is owned by Crayola.

SPAM

SPAM wasn't created specifically for World War II troops, but it became an integral part of their diet. The canned meat made of pork shoulder and ham was introduced in 1937 by Hormel Foods. It was designed to be an affordable, versatile meat product with a long shelf life that required no refrigeration – unique for its time. Hormel advertised SPAM aggressively in the early years, making it popular as a breakfast and lunch meat in American households.

During wartime, SPAM filled an even greater need: Not only did it continue to be eaten on the home front, it was embraced by the U.S. government, who bought 150 million pounds of SPAM to include in military menus. Ingenious soldiers discovered another use for SPAM – after they ate it, they used the grease from the cans to waterproof boots and lubricate weapons! (Never mind that the grease suggested the fat-laden content.) U.S. troops unwittingly turned SPAM into an international favorite by passing out tidbits to citizens of European and Asian countries.

After World War II, Hormel came up with the idea to promote SPAM via a musical troupe of female war veterans called the Hormel Girls. They traveled around the country and starred in their own radio show. A truly American innovation, SPAM has spawned fans in the United States and globally. Today, SPAM is a staple in Hawaii, a breakfast food in the Philippines, a holiday delicacy in South Korea and an American fast food as renowned as hamburgers in the United Kingdom. SPAM has even inspired its own museum and food festival.

Superman

Fictional comic book characters are strong personal brands who often embody traits that make them either loved or hated. Superman, arguably the world's most famous superhero, was the creation of two young men who liked to tell stories about heroes and villains in comic strip form. Jerry Siegel (writer) and Joe Shuster (artist) of Cleveland, Ohio first envisioned "Superman" as a villain in a comic strip, but they re-cast him as a superhero and sold the idea to National Periodical Publications. The premiere issue of "Action Comics" (June 1938) featured Superman.

At first, Superman only fought bad guys in America, but as war spread in Europe, he started engaging with thinly disguised European dictators. Until the U.S. entered the war, story lines didn't specifically mention Hitler, but it wasn't long before the Nazi leader was vilified in the pages of Action Comics. One of the more memorable covers was the July-August 1942 issue of Action Comics (Superman #17), which depicted Superman poised on Earth, firmly holding both Hitler and Hirohito by their necks. Superman quite literally fought for the Allies in World War II, at least in comic book form.

Superman played an educational role in the war as well. National Periodical Publications agreed to assist the War Department in producing special editions of Superman comic books especially for the military. Twenty-three issues were published to help soldiers, some of them illiterate, learn to read as well as for entertainment. The comic books also served as visual instructional manuals for operating machinery.

Superman may be the most famous superhero and one of the most enduring, but other American superheroes appeared during wartime. In fact, superheroes made comic books a convenient propaganda outlet for influencing children to support the American war effort. Batman debuted in May, 1939 in Detective Comics, and Captain America (who was created as a direct rebuke to Nazi Germany) first appeared in the March 1941 issue of Marvel's Captain America Comics.

Westinghouse
In the 1930s, Westinghouse, founded in 1886, had already achieved prominence as a diversified manufacturing and research firm involved in everything from radio to microwave to the Van de Graaff particle accelerator. The company made a major contribution to the war effort in multiple ways. The manufacturing side of Westinghouse produced in excess of 8,000 different products while its naval division developed turbine engines for naval vessels. In addition, Westinghouse Research Laboratories was responsible for innovations in atomic energy, plastics, radar, weapons and x-ray, as well as the first American-designed jet engine.

Westinghouse indirectly contributed to the "Rosie the Riveter" campaign, mentioned earlier. The company produced a poster featuring a woman worker with the headline, "We Can Do It!" The poster was displayed in several Westinghouse Electric plants as part of an internal advertising campaign designed to boost morale and encourage all workers, not just women, to function as a team. It was only after the war that this particular poster came to represent women war workers.

Because Westinghouse was known for its appliances, it did advertise frequently to consumers during the war, but the ads were largely institutional. For example, the company supported the government's national nutrition program through advertising and by creating its own "Health for Victory Clubs." In an ad employing the theme "Westinghouse makes a pledge," the company identified three different audiences – a seaman, a civilian war worker and a homemaker – whom Westinghouse pledged to support with excellent technology.

In the post-war years, Westinghouse was a leading defense contractor, constructed nuclear power plants, continued to produce consumer products and also got into television broadcasting.

Wrigley
The first stick chewing gum, made by Thomas Adams, appeared in 1870. However, it was in the late 1800s and early 1900s that chewing gum hit its stride. That's when Wrigley launched their Spearmint, Juicy Fruit and Doublemint flavors. It's also when Beech-Nut entered the gum market, Dentyne was concocted, Chiclets were invented and gumballs were introduced.

Wrigley's Doublemint was one of the better-known flavors during the war years due to the introduction in 1939 of the "Doublemint Twins." An ad campaign illustrated twins who loved the Doublemint flavor. The Doublemint Twins later appeared in photographs and on television.

When the U.S. military packaged its K-rations, a piece of chewing gum was included because of gum's ability to prevent mouth dryness, potentially aid digestion and reduce tension. The four flavors of gum used were Cinnamon, Peppermint, Spearmint and Wintergreen (also known as Pepsin). Gum was provided by American Chicle, Beech-Nut, Leaf Gum, Walla Walla and Wrigley. Wrigley's gum was produced in stick form, packaged in foil and covered in a brown wrapper. Some of the wrappers indicated "Army Ration."

Wrigley offered to pack K-rations and, of course, the company included its own brand of gum in the rations it handled – primarily Cinnamon and Spearmint. When other packing companies made up the K-rations, they would use a variety of gum brands. Gum was another one of those things American soldiers would hand out to foreign kids.

• CHAPTER 7 •

The Dark Side of World War Brands

After the Great War, the Treaty of Versailles included a provision demanding that Germany pay reparations that amounted to 132 billion gold marks – somewhere around $270 billion today.

Germany was in no position to meet its war obligations, so the Dawes Plan in 1924 reworked the reparations provision by reducing Germany's war debt and requiring the country to adopt a new currency. The United States played a unique role in the Dawes plan by lending Germany money to pay reparations to other countries, who then used the funds they received to pay back the United States. This unusual arrangement ultimately did not help to completely eliminate Germany's crushing debt. The onset of the Great Depression further pushed Germany's economy to the brink of collapse.

Hitler's rise to power achieved two things from an economic perspective: He arbitrarily cancelled Germany's war debt and he began to revive the German economy.

By the 1930s, American businesses were participating in a robust global economy that included Germany. Major American corporations with overseas operations often had foreign subsidiaries, some of which were in Germany. Perhaps American companies should have known better than to do business within Nazi Germany, but the greatly improving German economy presented a business opportunity some corporations saw as too good to pass up. As a result, several American companies did business in Germany and some actually assisted the German war effort, at least until America itself was engaged in war with Germany.

While it is easy to lay blame on these companies, they should not necessarily be regarded as traitorous. Even as they looked to profit from their operations in Germany, a fair number of them were important to America's war effort after the U.S. entered the war. When you read about the companies below, you'll see that they played a complex and sometimes contradictory role. War can result in business profits regardless of the wartime adversaries.

Here, then, is the dark side of World War brands: A sampling of American companies, and some foreign companies with close American connections, whose brands directly or indirectly supported Nazi Germany.

Associated Press

The Associated Press (AP) is a superpower media brand. Founded in 1846, the AP today has its own staff of journalists and also pools stories written by member newspapers, magazines, radio and television stations. While today it is a respected news organization, World War II was a time when the AP's integrity as an objective, trusted source of news was seriously called into question.

The Nazi regime brought with it an uncompromising attitude toward the dissemination of news and information. Any news organization in Nazi Germany had to abide by oppressive rules, essentially agreeing to publish Nazi propaganda and present Hitler and his acolytes in the best possible light. The Nazis also demanded that Jews be eliminated from newsroom staff.

Some international news organizations refused to comply and pulled out of the country. The AP, however, remained and did, in fact, terminate its local Jewish staff members. It also agreed to sanitize its reporting, eliminating or downplaying mention of the increasingly brutal acts committed against Jews and even declining to publish photographs that would incriminate the Nazis. By 1935, the AP was one of only a few international news organizations allowed to operate in Germany.

With America's entry into the war, the Berlin office of the AP was forced to close and American staff members were arrested and imprisoned. Despite this, the AP continued to work with other European countries to obtain photographs that were used by Nazi Germany in their propaganda.

Bayer

Bayer is a diversified global company that originated in Germany in 1863. Today Bayer has a large American presence and manufactures a wide range of products in pharmaceuticals, consumer health and crop science. Included in its brand portfolio are Aleve, Alka-Seltzer, Aspirin, Claritin, MiraLAX and One-a-Day.

Bayer's past is not to be applauded, though. It joined a chemical conglomerate in 1925 known as IG Farben. That firm was responsible for a number of wartime acts and atrocities, including guiding the Nazis in taking over chemical factories in Czechoslovakia and Poland. IG Farben's most notorious involvement in the war was its direct contribution to the Holocaust. The company suggested that its Zyklon-B insecticide, which contained cyanide, be used for Hitler's "final solution." It was Zyklon-B that was used to murder millions of men, women and children in Nazi gas chambers. IG Farben also used slave labor from Nazi concentration camps in its chemical factories.

While IG Farben's directors were indicted for war crimes after the war, only thirteen were convicted and all of them were released early. Fritz ter Meer, in charge of the Auschwitz IG Farben plant, became Bayer's president.

Eventually IG Farben was dissolved, and in 1952, Bayer became independent once again. Two other well-known companies that emerged from the disbanding of IG Farben were AGFA and BASF.

BMW

BMW (Bavarian Motor Works) is a German automobile and motorcycle manufacturer with a sterling reputation for luxury and quality. It is a very popular brand in the United States and maintains manufacturing facilities in America.

During World War II, however, Gunther Quandt, the patriarch of the Quandt family (major BMW stockholders), was so closely tied to Nazi Germany that Hitler called him the "Leader of the Defense Economy." In fact, BMW handsomely profited in Nazi Germany by using tens of thousands of concentration camp slave laborers to work for BMW plants manufacturing aircraft, vehicles and weapons. Gunther and his son Herbert Quandt also took advantage of the Nazi policy of seizing businesses from Jewish owners, taking them over as their own.

Contemporary Quandts had their family background researched. When Nazi ties were validated, the family acknowledged its past and BMW expressed its "profound regret" for the role the company played in the war.

Chanel

Earlier in this book, Chanel, founded by Gabrielle "Coco" Chanel, was cited as a leading French brand of the 1920s. What has come to light in recent years, due to the declassification of French World War II documents, is the unusual and unfortunate relationship Coco Chanel had with the Nazis.

Chanel was a celebrity fashion designer at the outbreak of World War II. While she was a friend of Winston Churchill, that didn't stop Chanel from associating with a German military officer named Baron Hans Günther von Dincklage after the Nazis took over Paris. Her romantic involvement with von Dincklage afforded her the ability to live comfortably in the Hotel Ritz even as her countrymen suffered from the invaders. Chanel also set her sights on recapturing her financial interest in her perfume business from the Wertheimers, a Jewish family who had invested in Chanel's perfumes and was now at risk.

Chanel continued her association with the Nazis and is said to have actually become one of their agents, although she denied it and managed to escape punishment in a French court of law. She made a triumphant return to fashion in 1954, ironically with the help of the Wertheimer family, and remained at the Hotel Ritz until her death in 1971.

Chase Bank
Chase has deep American roots – it was formed as Chase National Bank in 1877, became Chase Manhattan Bank in 1955, merged with Chemical Bank in 1995 and acquired JP Morgan in 2000. Additional mergers and acquisitions have created one of the world's leading financial institutions.

It is therefore embarrassing, and perhaps even scandalous, that Chase has been accused of freezing the accounts of its Jewish customers through its Paris office during World War II. In 1998, Chase said it was looking into whether its Paris office was "overly cooperative in providing banking services to Germany during the Occupation." Chase was also the bank behind Standard Oil (see below).

According to a Nov. 7, 1998 article in *The New York Times*, "Chase said it would consult with members of Jewish organizations and other experts to identify former customers of the Paris office of the Chase Bank or their heirs. If Chase discovers that the money was not returned after the war, it will pay its customers or their heirs with interest."

Fanta

Arguably one of the most all-American brands is Coca-Cola, and as mentioned earlier, Coca-Cola played a key role helping the American war effort. So is it possible that the Coca-Cola Company also had something to do with Nazi Germany? It did, but not directly.

By the 1930s and prior to the start of the war, Coca-Cola was popular worldwide, including in Germany. Germans were as crazy about Coke as Americans, and Coca-Cola GmbH, the German subsidiary, achieved record sales each year with the help of over forty bottling plants and hundreds of local distributors.

Coca-Cola GmbH wanted to maintain operations even after the war began, but it had a significant problem: It was not able to get the ingredients it needed to produce Coca-Cola syrup any longer since trade to Germany was for the most part embargoed by Great Britain. Max Keith, the head of the German operation, couldn't produce the Coca-Cola soda product, so he created another soft drink using ingredients that could be sourced locally. The soda was produced in a variety of fruit flavors, based on whatever ingredients were available at the time. Beet sugar was used as a sweetener.

As Keith brainstormed with his staff to conceive of a name for the new soda, he implored them to use their imaginations. Since the word for imagination in German is "Phantasie," a salesman suggested the word "Fanta." That's how the beverage got its name. Even as war raged, Coca-Cola GmbH was selling millions of cases of Fanta to German consumers.

Coca-Cola in America never controlled the German division during the war years; Keith worked independently but responsibly. When the war ended, he turned Fanta over to the Coca-Cola Company, along with the division's profits. Fanta was discontinued for a time but revived as an orange-flavored drink in 1955.

Ford
Ford is almost symbolic of the complex, contradictory relationship some American companies had with Nazi Germany. To begin with, the company's founder, Henry Ford, was revered by Adolph Hitler, who called Ford "my inspiration" and kept a portrait of him near his desk. Why did Ford, an American manufacturer, gain such respect from the notorious Nazi? Hitler was notably impressed with the automobile mass production innovations forged by Ford – but there is a darker reason. Hitler also embraced Ford's brazen anti-Semitism, which the American carmaker expressed in articles about "a vast Jewish conspiracy" published in The Dearborn Independent, owned by Ford.

Before the United States entered the war, Henry Ford was himself an admirer of Hitler and Nazi Germany. He even received the Grand Cross of the German Eagle, the highest medal Nazi Germany awarded to a foreigner.

The Ford Motor Company was no less important to the Nazi war machine. Ford's German division was building cars for Germany prior to the war, but its German manufacturing plants were repurposed during the war to manufacture military trucks. According to a Nov. 30, 1998 report in *The Washington Post,* war documents showed that General Motors (see below) and Ford "went along with the conversion of their German plants to military production at a time when U.S. government documents show they were still resisting calls by the Roosevelt administration to step up military production in their plants at home."

A 2001 report issued by Ford acknowledged that the company's German subsidiary, Ford-Werke, was indeed a functional component of the German war machine. As did other German companies, Ford-Werke used slave labor from a concentration camp to produce military materiel.

Even so, the Ford Motor Company played a key role helping the Allies after the United States entered the war, building a huge plant to manufacture B-24 Liberator bombers at the remarkable rate of one plane per hour. Ford produced almost 89,000 complete aircraft there. The company also made airplane engines, armored vehicles, generators, military gliders, jeeps and tanks at plants in the United States, Canada, Great Britain,

India, New Zealand and South Africa. Ironically, Henry Ford received the Distinguished Medal from the American Legion in 1944.

General Electric
General Electric (GE) was incorporated in 1889 as "Edison General Electric Company." Since then, GE has become a multi-division, multinational American corporation that, over the years, has been involved in aviation, consumer products, energy, finance and healthcare.

GE was indirectly involved in the previously mentioned Dawes Plan because one of its executives, Owen D. Young, was a U.S. delegate. In fact, U.S. loans made it possible for the German electrical industry to thrive under a firm called A.E.G., and GE was able to take a significant financial interest in the German company. GE also tried, unsuccessfully, to take an interest in Siemens, another major German manufacturer. By the time Hitler came to power, GE had four American directors on the board of A.E.G., effectively controlling the company.

Before the war, A.E.G. manufactured all sorts of consumer products, including irons, ovens, toasters and radiators. By 1942, however, the company was manufacturing products for Nazi Germany's wartime needs. A.E.G. was also found to have contributed to the political fund of Adolph Hitler. German directors of A.E.G. were held accountable for war crimes but the American directors were not.

When the United States entered the war, General Electric in the U.S. worked on behalf of the American war effort. Some of its executives assisted the military, and the company's manufacturing plants produced war materiel. GE had already developed the turbosupercharger, which was used in World War II airplanes flying at higher altitudes and carrying heavier payloads. GE also built America's first jet engine for the military, but it was not ready to be deployed until after the war ended.

General Motors
General Motors (GM) was, like Ford, another American automobile manufacturer with a "Nazi problem." Bradford Snell, a staff attorney for the U.S. Senate Judiciary Committee, issued a report in 1974 that identified GM and its Opel division as colluding with the Nazis. According to *The Washington Post*, Snell said, "General Motors was far more important to the Nazi war machine than Switzerland. Switzerland was just a repository of looted funds. GM was an integral part of the German war effort. The Nazis could have invaded Poland and Russia without Switzerland. They could not have done so without GM."

General Motors has been less forthcoming than Ford about its role in assisting Nazi Germany, indicating that the company lost control of its German plants during the war. Still, GM provided synthetic fuel technology that enabled Germany to invade Poland and built Nazi warplanes through its Opel division. According to *The Washington Post*, James Mooney, the American director of overseas operations for GM, knew of and was involved in the conversion of a German automobile plant to produce war materiel.

Like its competitor Ford, however, after the United States entered the war, GM's activities on the home front were unwaveringly patriotic and unassailable. Its many divisions and production plants were crucial to American war efforts, manufacturing millions of miscellaneous parts, as well as aircraft engines, cannon, machine guns, naval fighters and torpedo bombers, tanks, tank destroyers and trucks.

Hugo Boss
Hugo Boss, whose brand name is BOSS, is a German maker of luxury clothing, footwear, fragrances and accessories. As one of Germany's largest fashion companies, it is a well-known brand in the United States. What may not be widely recognized, however, is that the company's founder, Hugo Boss, was a Nazi. After he started his company in 1924, Boss watched the rise of Hitler in Germany and promptly decided to manufacture uniforms for the Nazis. Boss joined the Nazi party and was an active supporter of their policies, which gave him preferential treatment in obtaining contracts. His young company ended up producing uniforms for the Nazi SA storm troopers, the SS, and the Hitler Youth, as well as the German military and rail and postal workers.

With such a thriving business, Boss needed many more workers. He didn't hesitate to make use of slave workers from countries invaded by Germany, including France and Poland. Working conditions in Boss' factories were said to be horrendous.

When the war ended, Hugo Boss was not only fined for his role, he was forbidden from continuing to own a business in Germany. As a result, Boss transferred the ownership of the company to his son-in-law. It wasn't until 1999 that the firm agreed to compensate former slave workers through a special fund.

IBM

IBM started its corporate life as a company called Computing-Tabulating-Recording Company (CTR). It specialized in tabulating data using punch cards and was renamed International Business Machines (IBM) in 1924 by its then president, Thomas J. Watson. A proponent of international trade, Watson was president of the International Chamber of Commerce and grew IBM into a global powerhouse by the 1930s. In fact, IBM's most profitable operation outside the United States was Dehomag, its German subsidiary.

Watson himself met with Hitler. As a result, IBM developed a relationship with Nazi Germany to the extent that the company supplied the punch card technology used to conduct a census. The census was nothing more than a thinly veiled excuse to identify and track "undesirables," such as Jews and Gypsies, so they could be exterminated by the Nazis. The system kept tabs on millions of individuals, tracking them from their homes and workplaces to concentration and extermination camps. The Nazis were scrupulous record-keepers; IBM's technology was even used to identify where each individual was sent and how each one died.

Even after it was apparent that the system was being used for the Holocaust, IBM continued to supply Germany with machines. With the entry of the United States into the war in 1941, Dehomag was seized and controlled by German shareholders, and IBM's U.S. operations began to provide data processing equipment to help the American war effort. However, an exhaustively researched book published in 2001 (*IBM and the Holocaust* by Edwin Black) revealed that at the same time the American headquarters was working on behalf of the United States, IBM subsidiaries in Europe still delivered punch cards to Nazi Germany, and IBM executives directed operations through neutral Switzerland.

Kodak

The Eastman Kodak Company, better known as "Kodak," was synonymous with cameras and photographic film for over one hundred years. Henry Strong and George Eastman founded the company in 1888, and Eastman was the first to create a simple camera, the Instamatic, that all consumers could use. Kodak was a photographic powerhouse until the digital revolution contributed to its bankruptcy in 2012.

Before the start of World War II, Kodak, like many leading American companies, ran numerous European operations. Kodak's German subsidiary was taken over by the Nazis in much the same way as other American corporate subsidiaries, but Kodak found a work around: Executives at the American Kodak headquarters developed a relationship with Wilhelm Keppler, economic adviser to Adolph Hitler, enabling them to maintain informal control of the German subsidiary. What's more, Kodak continued to do business with Nazi Germany even after America entered the war. How? By routing products, supplies and cash through its operations in Portugal, Spain and Switzerland.

Kodak's German subsidiary actually expanded its operations during World War II, using slave labor to manufacture military materiel for Nazi Germany. Kodak's French subsidiary also continued operating while under Nazi control. When Kodak took back management of both the German and French subsidiaries after the war, the company was flush with profits from its Nazi endeavors. Kodak failed to apologize for its wartime role but did contribute to a fund for families of slave laborers.

Nestlé

As mentioned previously, Nestlé's Nescafé brand of instant coffee was very popular with both American civilians and military personnel during World War II. Nestlé itself was founded in Switzerland by a German-born pharmacist, Henri Nestlé, who developed an early baby formula. By 1905, he agreed to merge his company with a U.S. company, Anglo-Swiss Condensed Milk. The merged company ultimately became the modern-day Nestlé, probably best known for its chocolate.

Switzerland's neutrality, as well as its American connection, likely helped the company continue to do business during World War II. When war broke out in Europe, the company opened a new U.S. office that effectively functioned as corporate headquarters. Since Nestlé could not export its products from Europe, it did so from the United States and Australia, expanding its production facilities into Latin America.

Nestlé did not work directly with the Nazis, although its chocolate bars were a favorite of Nazi soldiers, who handed them out to Jewish children as a form of entrapment. In addition, Maggi, a Swiss soup maker acquired by Nestlé shortly after the war ended, was a known user of slave labor from Germany's concentration camps. To its credit, Nestlé contributed over $14 million to a Holocaust survivors fund.

Siemens
Siemens was founded by Werner von Siemens in Germany in 1847. Today it has a substantial U.S. presence and has grown into a global industrial powerhouse in numerous areas, including energy, finance, healthcare and industrial automation. Like other German companies, Siemens prospered under the Nazi regime. As the leader in the German electrical industry, Siemens profited from the war, even though the company claims the head of Siemens from 1933 to 1941, Carl Friedrich von Siemens, "detested the Nazi dictatorship."

Siemens faced a difficult worker shortage during the war because many employees at its plants were drafted into the military. From 1943 until the end of the war, the company was pressed to fill the need for wartime electrical equipment and had to use slave labor to do so. According to Siemens, "These laborers included people from territories occupied by the German military, prisoners of war, Jews, Sinti, Roma and, in the final phase of the war, concentration camp inmates. During the entire period from 1940 to 1945, at least 80,000 forced laborers worked at Siemens."

Siemens was compelled to forfeit eighty percent of its total worth at the end of the war and was faced with a lengthy rebuilding process. Still, Siemens has acknowledged its wrongdoing and accepted responsibility for its wartime role. Since 1962, Siemens has made tens of millions of dollars of contributions to various funds. In addition, today it works with the Ravensbrück concentration camp memorial site to educate its employees through on-premises programs.

Standard Oil

Before the existence of such familiar oil industry names as Amoco, BP, Chevron, Exxon Mobil and Shell there was Standard Oil. This oil-producing American behemoth, founded in 1870 by John D. Rockefeller and Henry Flagler, became the world's largest refiner of oil before it was deemed an illegal monopoly by the U.S. government in 1911. The result of that landmark decision was to divide Standard Oil into 34 smaller but still significant oil companies. Two of them, Standard Oil of New Jersey and Standard Oil of New York, eventually became Esso/Exxon and Mobil, respectively.

By 1941, Standard Oil of New Jersey had virtually become a monopoly again, responsible for eighty-four percent of the U.S. petroleum market. Oil was such a critical resource during World War II that both sides, the Allies and the Axis countries, desperately needed it. The two largest stockholders of Standard Oil of New Jersey at the time were the Rockefeller family and none other than German giant IG Farben, which played a major role in supporting the Nazi regime. (See Bayer above.) It was only natural that Standard Oil became a supplier to Nazi Germany.

Prior to the United States entering the war, Standard Oil actively assisted the Nazis with technology that allowed them to produce synthetic gasoline from coal. This was crucial because, while Nazi Germany had rich coal resources, they had little access to crude petroleum. In addition, Standard Oil, along with other companies, provided the tetraethyl lead gasoline necessary for planes of the German air force, the Luftwaffe. As such, Standard Oil literally fueled the Nazi war machine.

Standard Oil of New Jersey and Standard Oil of California engaged in wartime deception when their oil tankers were re-registered under the flag of Panama, enabling the ships to evade search or seizure by the British navy. According to a March 31, 1941 U.S. State Department report, these tankers carried oil that was eventually delivered to Nazi Germany. Standard Oil also provided tetraethyl lead to Japan.

When the United States entered the war, Standard Oil provided petroleum products to the Allies as well. However, Standard Oil's role in helping Nazi Germany may have continued throughout the war were it not for the publication of a book entitled *Sequel to the Apocalypse* by "John Boylan" that exposed the company's relationship with the Nazis. Reportedly, the book was actually authored by Nelson A. Rockefeller, grandson of

Standard Oil's founder, John D. Rockefeller, to make amends for the family's wartime involvement with Axis powers.

Volkswagen

The German company Volkswagen is one of the world's largest automobile manufacturers. Its most iconic model, the "Beetle," became a sensation in the America of the 1960s, when Boomers adopted it as a symbol of the "flower power" generation. The VW bus was also renowned during that era as a hippie-friendly vehicle. Little did the peace-and-love generation know that the Beetle was a Nazi creation.

The company's beginnings are linked to a dark history. When Hitler came to power in Germany, most cars were luxury models, unaffordable by ordinary citizens. Hitler thought common folk needed their own cheap vehicle, so he worked directly with Ferdinand Porsche (yes, *that* Porsche) to develop a "people's car," whose translation into German is "volks wagen." Porsche created the "Volksauto," a small round-shaped automobile with an air-cooled rear engine that could be manufactured inexpensively. It was the forerunner of the Beetle.

Enthusiastic about the Volksauto, Hitler proposed that the government subsidize its production, making it possible for every German family to own a car. He even created a new town, Wolfsburg, to house a factory and its workers. The plan was short lived, however. When Nazi Germany started the war in Europe, the Volkswagen factory was repurposed to manufacture military vehicles. Ferdinand Porsche designed many of them, including the popular Volkswagen Kübelwagen, a Jeep-like vehicle. Production of the Volksauto continued as well, but it was used mostly by Nazi government officials rather than consumers.

Volkswagen was reviled once the war ended. American, British and French automobile manufacturers were offered the opportunity to acquire the company but none of them wanted it. Instead, Volkswagen remained in German hands and again began to produce the Beetle in 1946. A symbol of the rise of the new West German economy, Volkswagen went on to become a global automobile manufacturer headquartered in Wolfsburg. Its brand portfolio today includes Audi, Bentley, Bugatti, Ducati, Lamborghini, Porsche and Volkswagen.

• PART III •

The Birth of the Modern American Brand

• CHAPTER 8 •

The Consumer in Post-War America

The war economy had brought an abrupt end to the Great Depression. American manufacturing had turned its attention to converting consumer product plants into a vast wartime production machine. Americans who didn't directly fight in the war enthusiastically supported the war effort on the home front by working in manufacturing plants to produce war materiel or volunteering with organizations such as the American Red Cross and United Service Organizations (USO). By 1944, the unemployment rate in the United States was just 1.2 percent as compared to 14.6 percent in 1939 and 25 percent during the height of the Great Depression. The cynical statement, "War is good business," was never truer for the United States than during World War II.

When the war ended with an Allied victory, the United States had much to celebrate. Everyone believed that good triumphed over evil. While 300,000 members of the American armed forces were killed in battle, the death toll was considerably less than in any other country. In addition, the United States was spared the physical horror of a war that left Europe in shambles and Japan devastated by two American atomic bombs.

Some observers were cynical of the country's ability to reverse course and return to a peacetime economy, but American industry managed to execute a miraculously rapid transition, returning factories from wartime to consumer production. The reason was compelling: American consumers, who had patiently lived with food rationing, resource conservation and product shortages during the war years were now ready to get back to their daily lives. In fact, Americans had sacrificed during the war, spending less and generally saving more of their money. The result was a pent-up demand for consumer products of all kinds. It turns out that those marketers who made the decision to maintain their brands' awareness through wartime advertising benefitted from this emerging consumerism.

Post-war America was ripe with promise and opportunity, and consumers responded accordingly. The 1944 GI Bill of Rights encouraged returning servicemen to enroll in college, purchase homes, buy farms and start families. The year 1946 is widely regarded as the start of the "Baby Boom," which would last until 1964. During this period, tens of millions of children were born, largely to families in the growing middle class.

Not everyone had the same advantages from the postwar economy, however. African Americans who fought in the war still faced segregation, discrimination and injustice when they returned home. Women who had valiantly worked at "men's jobs" on the home front were expected to return to their role as unpaid homemakers. African Americans and women were essentially thrown back into their same pre-war socioeconomic status without much improvement.

The war-weary American public also had a new geopolitical threat to worry about: The Cold War. Only a short time after the end of World War II, communism was on the rise in Russia and China. Korea had been separated into North and South Korea. With the communist North supported by Russia and the non-communist South backed by the United States, hostilities broke out. The 1950 Korean War resulted in 40,000 American deaths before an armistice was reached in 1953. Americans didn't have much enthusiasm for another conflict, so it was a good thing the Korean War was short-lived. Communism remained entrenched, however, and it became the center of a "red scare" perpetrated primarily by an American senator, Joseph McCarthy.

Still, even the threat of communism failed to get in the way of Americans' focus on upward mobility. The middle class began to spread beyond city centers into suburbia. Levittown, a development of residential homes constructed on former farmland in Long Island, New York in 1947, is believed to be the first true American suburb. Look-alike homes were quickly built to accommodate families, but they were restricted to whites only.

My own family was a typical example of the suburban migration. My mother and father were second generation Americans; their parents had come to America as immigrants from Russia and Poland. My mother's parents lived with us. My father, an obstetrician, set aside his professional practice to become a medical officer in the United States Army during World War II. When he returned to our home in Brooklyn, New York after the war, my parents were ready to participate in a more prosperous American society. I was born in Brooklyn during the Baby Boom in 1948. Not long after, my parents decided to follow the herd to suburbia and move to a home on Long Island. They later relocated to a residential area in Queens where I spent the remainder of my childhood.

The suburban migration brought with it new ways to shop, including supermarkets and shopping centers, complete with sprawling parking lots. In the four years after the war (1945 – 1949), Americans bought over 21 million cars, 20 million refrigerators and over 5 million stoves. By the mid-1950s, despite a 1953-54 recession, over half of Americans were enjoying a standard of living defined as solidly middle class. By the decade's end, 60 percent of Americans owned homes, 75 percent owned at least one automobile and 87 percent owned at least one television.

A look at U.S. Bureau of Labor Statistics current consumption data for wage and clerical workers in urban households demonstrates the growth in consumer income and spending for 1950 as compared to 1941, the first year of the war. Total after-tax income was $3,910 in 1950 vs. $2,372 in 1941. Consumption was

$3,808 in 1950 vs. $2,060 in 1941. Food including alcohol was $1,195 in 1950 vs. $637 in 1941. Total housing was $1,035 in 1950 vs. $598 in 1941.

The country's Gross National Product (GNP), $200 billion in 1940, reached $300 billion by 1950 and over $500 billion by 1960. America was quickly growing into an economic superpower: By 1955, the United States, with only 6 percent of the world's population, was responsible for almost half of the goods produced by the world's nations.

Post-war Americans exhibited buying behavior that was the polar opposite of the war years. Instead of conserving and sacrificing, Americans were becoming keen consumers with an unquenchable desire for material goods. They were interested in lavishing themselves with modern conveniences and new products. It was almost as if the whole society was enjoying the spoils of war – but it was really part of a post-war economic boom.

"Buying American" was seen as patriotic and a way to sustain economic recovery. Americans were even willing to purchase goods on revolving credit, primarily with oil company and department stores charge cards. Combined with home mortgages, that led to a new attitude toward the concept of credit. In 1950, the first general purpose charge card was introduced by Diner's Club, followed shortly thereafter by charge cards from Carte Blanche and American Express. The consumer credit revolution really exploded in 1958 when "BankAmericard," the first true bank credit card, came to market courtesy of Bank of

America in California. That foray into bank credit cards eventually led to the birth in the 1960s of VISA and MasterCard, two financial organizations that backed national credit cards issued by individual banks. Consumer debt increased from just under $6 million in 1945 to just over $56 billion in 1960.

The urgent need for certain materials during the war had created changes in consumer products, so Americans had learned to adjust to new kinds of product packaging. For example, with tin in short supply, many cans were replaced with glass jars or cardboard cartons. Any consumer product that used a petroleum-based ingredient had to be reformulated. Even currency was modified: Zinc was substituted for copper in pennies. While some of these changes endured, manufacturers were relieved to see a revived supply of the substances they needed to return to the original packaging of consumer products.

Some positive outcomes from the war had an impact on consumer packaged goods. Wartime product innovations invaded everyday living in post-war America. Nylon, originally consigned to war use, regained its position as an important material used in stockings and clothing, as well as for industrial applications. Frozen orange juice, the result of wartime experimentation, was introduced into the consumer market. The aerosol spray can, perfected during the war so soldiers could deter insects carrying malaria, was repurposed, first for hair spray and eventually for deodorant and other consumer products.

Plastic came of age during the war and post-war years. Previously used for upscale products, plastic was needed during the war years for more ordinary uses. As a result, plastic was perceived at that time as something of an inferior substitute for packaging material. To fight this lingering wartime perception, the plastics industry boasted about "the wonders of plastic" to the public in 1946 via the first National Plastics Exposition held in New York City. Some 87,000 people attended, marveling at the ways in which plastic could be used to improve modern life. They saw everything from window screens to artificial flowers to kitchen countertops to clear plastic that would reveal what was inside any package. The use of plastic in such diverse products as vinyl siding for homes, food wrap, squeeze bottles and toys soon became commonplace. One of the notable plastic brands of the 1950s was Tupperware, enthusiastically embraced by homemakers.

The mindset of Americans was changing. Now consumers were more than happy to overlook the permanence of the past. Instead, they embraced disposability. It is no accident that the "Keep America Beautiful" campaign launched in 1953. Created by the Ad Council, which was a post-war outgrowth of the wartime War Advertising Council, this public service campaign focused attention on litter, which was becoming a national embarrassment.

The business community unashamedly adopted the same disposability mentality. Clothing fashions changed annually, as did car models. Manufacturers of every type took note and began to employ the "model year" strategy for consumer products.

"New and improved" products appeared on an annual basis. The post-war years became an era of planned obsolescence, creating a new problem that would continue for decades: an excess of garbage.

"Bigger and better" was a sign of the times, even pervading the sports world. The public adored America's national pastime, baseball. Fans were stunned when, in 1957, owners of National League baseball teams approved of moving two teams from New York City to the land of fun and sun, California – the New York Giants to San Francisco and the Brooklyn Dodgers to Los Angeles. Both teams were convinced they could expand their fan base and generate more revenue by heading West. Los Angeles promised to build a much bigger stadium for the Dodgers to play in, but seeing the beloved "bums" leave Brooklyn's quaint, homey Ebbets Field was a bitter pill to swallow for Brooklynites.

Another interesting side effect of the war was the more than $30 billion worth of surplus U.S. military goods left over after the Allied victory. Some materials could be repurposed into consumer products and other items were prized by collectors of wartime memorabilia. Still, there was such a glut of military goods that it led Army-Navy surplus stores to spring up around the nation. Ironically, the bell bottoms and military jackets sold there became the garments of choice for hippies and anti-war protestors of the 1960s and 1970s.

The Car Culture

One of the most telling signs of a changing economy was the new emphasis on travel. While commercial air travel had been available to wealthier consumers before and during the war, it really began to take off during the 1950s. Interest in air travel surged as domestic airlines including American, Eastern, Pan American, Trans World (TWA) and United faced growing competition. The Civil Aeronautics Board was created to set airline routes and fares.

But it was automobile travel that gained the most traction. Just about every American family was interested in purchasing a car, and the American automobile industry was delighted to meet the national need. After a wartime materiel production spree, Detroit retooled its factories to focus on cars again. As a result, America's automobile industry grew into the world's largest, supporting one in six American jobs. More than eight million cars were manufactured in 1950 alone. By 1958, more than sixty-seven million automobiles were registered in the country.

The Interstate Highway System included about 10,000 miles of road surface by 1960 upon which Americans could drive across country, from north to south and from east to west. Most families took road trips for their summer vacations. Just as important, the interstate network of national roads (today about 45,000 miles) contributed to the country's economic expansion. Gas stations, restaurants and motels popped up along the highways, goods could be transported nationwide via trucks and American families enjoyed greater flexibility in terms of where they could live, work and play.

The car culture of America in the 1950s dramatically influenced the way in which people traveled, shopped and ate. "Cruisin'" the streets at night was a popular teen pastime. NASCAR ran its first race in 1948. The automobile was celebrated in songs, magazines, books, television shows and movies.

The automobile's pervasiveness gave rise to an entire range of businesses, including drive-in movies, drive-in and fast-food restaurants, shopping centers, roadside motel chains, car washes and the like. The first drive-thru wedding chapel opened in Las Vegas in 1951. Howard Johnson, created in 1925, became the country's most formidable roadside restaurant chain during the 1950s. At its height, Howard Johnson had over 1,000 restaurants. Howard Johnson Motor Lodges, added in 1954, enhanced the company's brand awareness.

The late 1940s and 1950s saw the creation of such powerhouse national travel, food and retail brands as Best Western, Burger King, Denny's, Dick's Sporting Goods, Dunkin' Donuts, Holiday Inn, Jersey Mike's, Kentucky Fried Chicken, McDonald's, Pizza Hut, Sonic, Taco Bell, Toys 'R Us and U-Haul.

The "Big Three" automakers – Chrysler, Ford and General Motors – dominated the automobile industry, producing an almost endless line of car brands and models, typically updated annually. Cars manufactured for families were ubiquitous – station wagons were especially popular. But other styles began to emerge in the 1950s and 1960s, such as sports cars and high-performance "muscle" cars. Technology and styling were equally showcased as automakers fought for market share.

Here are a few of the iconic automobile brands of the time:

Cadillac
This General Motors (GM) luxury brand pulled out all the stops with its 1959 model, best known for its oversize tail fins and bullet taillamps. Pioneered by Cadillac, the tail fin was modeled after a jet airplane stabilizer. The 1959 Cadillac also featured outstanding visibility due to a wraparound windshield. It included automatic transmission, power steering and power brakes as standard equipment.

"Chevy"
Dinah Shore crooning "See the USA in Your Chevrolet" on her television show helped make this GM brand a household word, even though its nickname, "Chevy," was the preferred moniker. The 1957 Chevy is thought to be the world's most classic car – still commonly seen on the streets of Havana, Cuba. The car's wide front grille, bumper bullets and chrome headlines gave the model its human face-like appearance. Sitting low to the ground, the Chevy was the first model to have tubeless tires. This car was recognized by fans as a dependable NASCAR and Daytona 500 competitor.

Corvette

The Chevrolet Corvette, GM's first sports car model, created such buzz that production started in mid-1953, just six months after it was unveiled to enthusiastic car buffs. A favorite of consumers and race car drivers alike, the "Vette," as it was commonly known, quickly entered a class all its own. The car became even more popular in 1963 with the introduction of the Corvette Sting Ray.

Edsel

The launch of the Edsel in 1957 marked a low point for Ford. Despite being exhaustively researched and positioned as "the car of the future," this unattractive auto was the wrong car at the wrong time. The high price, coupled with the fact that compact cars unlike the mid-sized Edsel were piquing the interest of American drivers, spelled doom for this unlucky Ford brand.

GTO

The GTO, from the Pontiac division of General Motors, didn't come along until 1964, but it is worthy of mention because it is credited with starting the "muscle car" craze. This "souped up" version of the Tempest brand family featured a larger engine in a lighter body, even though technically, it wasn't a racing car. One of its designers was John DeLorean, who started his own car company in 1975.

Mustang

Another 1964 car brand that should be acknowledged is the Ford Mustang. It was considered the first "pony car," a term accorded cars that were small, sporty and affordable. The very year it was introduced, the Mustang was the pace car in the Indianapolis 500 and it appeared in "Goldfinger," a James Bond film. In 1968, Steve McQueen famously drove a Mustang in the movie, "Bullitt."

Thunderbird

The 1955 introduction of the Thunderbird, originally a two-seat convertible, heralded the onset of an iconic brand designed specifically by Ford to compete with the Corvette. The Thunderbird did outsell the Vette in its early years, but the model was upgraded and enlarged by 1958 when a rear seat was added. Often called the "T-Bird," the Thunderbird evolved into a classic luxury car brand.

• CHAPTER 9 •

The Era of Television

The technology that began to emerge in the post-war era may seem tame by comparison to modern technological innovations, but it was revolutionary for its time. Less essential technological inventions were focused on entertainment: The "View-Master," a three-dimensional viewing device created in 1939, became popular in the 1950s. The 45 RPM record, first issued by RCA Victor in 1949, is credited with bringing rock 'n' roll to the youth of America. The transistor radio, introduced in 1954, made it possible for consumers to hear radio stations anywhere, including in automobiles.

Advancements in other areas of technology were more significant: The Polaroid Land camera, launched in 1948, pioneered instant photography, eventually leading to full-color instant photos by 1963 – a physical precursor to digital photography. In 1951, the first commercial computer was brought to market by UNIVAC. The industrial strength plain paper copier that Xerox introduced in 1959 revolutionized duplication and was the forerunner of desktop copiers. The first commercial jet airliner, the de Havilland DH 106 Comet, was put into service in 1952, marking the inception of jet travel. The first trans-Atlantic telephone cable was operational in 1956. In 1963, the rotary dial telephone was replaced with the Bell System's "Touch-Tone" technology, which became a worldwide standard.

From a consumer and certainly a branding perspective, though, the most important technological innovation of the post-war era was television. Although the birth of commercial television is most closely associated with post-war America, the first use of experimental broadcast television actually occurred in 1928. Television was introduced to the public at the 1939 New York World's Fair. Television broadcasting was used sporadically after that, but it wasn't until the Federal Communications Commission established television standards in 1941 that commercial television broadcasting was viable. That year, a television test pattern that looked like a clock with a moving minute hand was broadcast on a New York TV station. A logo for Bulova, and the phrase "Bulova Watch Time," accompanied the graphic. This was believed to be the very first television commercial.

Radio remained the dominant medium through the end of World War II; there were some 40 million radios nationwide in 1947, compared with around 44,000 television sets. Early on, televisions were expensive and television broadcasting stations were few and far between. Still, television grew in popularity by the end of the decade, with such ground-breaking networks as Columbia Broadcasting System (CBS) and National Broadcasting Corporation (NBC), (*Appendix, 26*) and later the American Broadcasting Corporation (ABC), providing most of the programming. By 1950, Americans had purchased five million television sets. While less than 20 percent of American households had a TV in 1950, almost 90 percent of homes had at least one in 1960.

Television didn't supplant radio as a medium as much as supplement it. In fact, radio networks made the transition to television while retaining their radio roots. Like radio, television was "free" to the public, but that did not mean free of advertising; on the contrary, revenue from advertisers is what kept both radio and television operating at no cost to consumers. Also like radio, television was not merely an entertainment medium – it ultimately became a vital source of world, national and local news, with the added benefit of visuals to go along with a news reporter's verbal narrative.

Soap operas easily made the transition from radio to television, as did variety, adventure, comedy and game shows. Television shows reflected the cultural and societal norms of the time. For example, "Amos 'n' Andy" was an extremely popular comedy show that began on radio in 1928. Although writers/actors Freeman Gosden and Charles Correll were white, the show chronicled the antics of Black characters. Despite the fact that the content was overtly racist, "Amos 'n' Andy" switched to television in 1951, using Black actors in comedy skits that were insulting to Blacks. The TV series was short-lived, largely due to a legitimate protest lodged by the NAACP. Although the show was cancelled, it still went into syndicated reruns until 1966.

"Amos 'n' Andy" was typical of one of the most popular and commercially successful television show formats: the "sitcom." Other early sitcoms included "The Goldbergs," about a Jewish New York family, "The Honeymooners," featuring Jackie Gleason as a New York bus driver, and the perennial favorite, "The Adventures of Ozzie and Harriet," which followed the semi-fictional life of the Nelson family from 1952 to 1966.

Television programming was divided into three basic time segments: Daytime, Primetime (evenings) and Weekends; Saturday mornings were devoted to children's programming. This segmentation made it simpler for advertisers to reach target audiences, specifically housewives during the daytime, families during primetime and children on Saturday mornings.

Any kid who grew up in the 1950s has fond memories of Saturday morning TV. Boomer kids of all ages had a wonderful potpourri of programs from which to choose – cartoons, science fiction, comedy, adventure, Westerns and more. Whether it was Annie Oakley, Bugs Bunny, Captain Midnight, The Lone Ranger, Mr. Wizard, Rin Tin Tin, Roy Rogers or Superman, each child had his or her favorite shows and heroes.

Of all the advertising on television, the commercials and product placements directly targeting children were likely the most controversial. Every kid watching Saturday morning television had a steady diet of blatant product promotions and hard-sell TV commercials. After all, kids of the '50s were part of the postwar affluent middle class; they were an attractive audience that advertisers rightly saw as influencing the purchasing behavior of their parents.

Saturday morning television programs were themselves brands of a sort. Each show had its own timeslot, name, brand platform, distinct typeface, original song and branded characters or personalities who were only too happy to pitch products. Cereal, snack food, soft drinks, toys and clothing were all advertised directly to children; at times, products were cleverly if insidiously woven right into the content of the show – the forerunner of a practice today called "product placement."

The local television channels and television networks were well aware of the compelling fact that, without advertisers' dollars, there would be no television programming – and that included children's programming. Saturday morning television, along with the accompanying commercials, remained a staple for children until children's television programming was modified by the 1990 Children's Television Act.

The Super Brand Booster

Before the advent of television, brand marketers depended on a combination of newspaper, magazine and radio advertising to pitch their products to the American consumer. For more elaborate campaigns, brand advertisers may have added in-store product promotions, outdoor advertising (billboards, posters, buses, etc.) and filmed commercials that ran in movie theaters.

The importance of television to brand marketers cannot be over-stated. Television was the rocket fuel that propelled the media strategy for virtually every brand. As television grew into the dominant medium throughout the 1950s and into the 1960s, brand marketers recognized that they could reach a vast audience with their commercial messages. Since television was an audiovisual medium, it bested both print and radio by combining the written word with sound, visuals, animation and live action.

One of the lesser-known facts about those vanguard television advertisers is the creative control they exerted in the 1950s. During the early years of television, advertising agencies for major brands produced not only television commercials but often the shows themselves. It wasn't unusual for a major advertiser to influence the products shown (or not shown) and even to have input into the show's script. Advertisers' products were often incorporated into the shows. Anything controversial or of questionable taste was sure to be censored by the advertiser. Television programs were frequently interrupted by commercials.

Early television shows were often sponsored by companies; the advertiser's brand name would become a prominent part of the show, such as "The Colgate Comedy Hour," "General Electric Theater," "Philco TV Playhouse" and "Texaco Star Theatre." Most early shows were sponsored by just one brand with no competitors allowed; it was only after networks started controlling the programming that multiple brands, even competitors, could advertise during each television show.

Early television commercials were either filmed or performed live. Television and movie celebrities were often hired as spokespeople. Sometimes personalities of particular shows promoted products in separate commercials or during the show itself. Advertising jingles (short, catchy songs that accompanied product pitches) transitioned from radio to television, becoming all the more memorable when they were integrated with visual images.

Animation was a popular technique utilized in many early commercials. Iconic cartoon mascots, such as Bucky Beaver (Ipana toothpaste), Speedy (Alka-Seltzer) and Tony the Tiger (Kellogg's Frosted Flakes) were specially created to pitch products. Well-known animated characters also shilled for advertisers; for example, Rocky and Bullwinkle of The Rocky and Bullwinkle Show were spokes-animals for the entire line of cereals from General Mills, while Fred and Barney of The Flintstones television series puffed away on Winston cigarettes.

Popular television shows first attracted thousands and eventually millions of viewers, providing national advertisers with a tantalizingly large audience for their products. Local television stations offered attractive, reasonably priced commercial airtime for area retailers, such as car dealers, hardware stores and restaurants.

In many respects, brand advertising was much easier in the early days of television. Television commercials were limited to running during advertiser-produced shows or the shows created by three major networks, along with some local programming. It was nothing like the countless shows on hundreds of cable, satellite and streaming channels available today. Advertisers were also restricted to black-and-white commercials until color television became more widely available in the mid 1960s.

From the outset, television was a super brand booster, gaining a foothold as the dominant American medium. Numerous consumer brands became timeless classics thanks in large part to television. Here is a sampling of post-war brands that achieved high awareness during the early years of television (late 1940s, 1950s and early 1960s).

Classic Brands of Early Television

Automobiles and Gasoline
Several iconic American automobile brands were mentioned earlier, but it's important to note that automobiles and automobile-related products played a prominent role in early television commercials. Americans of the era adored cars, and being on the road was increasingly common for work and for play. American carmakers answered the call by being some of the most active television advertisers.

Chevrolet
No car brand was more prominent than Chevrolet in the early days of television. By 1933, one out of every three vehicles sold in the United States was a Chevy. While World War II disrupted the production of Chevrolet's parent company, General Motors (along with every other car manufacturer), automobiles made a

quick comeback. Chevrolet was one of the first brands to use television advertising; as early as 1946, Chevrolet sponsored variety shows that appeared in four cities. In 1948, Chevrolet's first national television commercial ran, well before TV was a widely adopted household medium. Even then the jingle, "See the USA in Your Chevrolet," was being used. In 1950, the brand reportedly invested more in advertising than any other automobile brand – a total of $51 million, which included a mix of television, print, radio and outdoor. The next year, Chevrolet began a sponsorship of "The Dinah Shore Show" that would last for ten years. Shore sang the timeless jingle during her show and in stand-alone commercials. In 1957, the first color television commercial appeared for Chevrolet. The brand continues to make heavy use of television to this day.

Hertz
Walter Jacobs rented Model-Ts as early as 1918, but in 1923, he sold his fledgling company to John D. Hertz. By 1925, The Hertz Corporation had established a national rental network, and in 1932, it opened the first rental car facility at an airport. Hertz was well ahead of the rental market, which became all the more profitable during the car culture of the 1950s. Hertz was the market leader in the U.S., and by 1955, Hertz was the first car rental company to have 1,000 locations worldwide. In 1959, an ad agency for Hertz came up with the tag line, "Let Hertz Put You in the Driver's Seat." This memorable slogan was set to catchy music in the early 1960s. It led to the creation of a classic television commercial, using special effects to show a male driver and his female companion floating in air as they plop down into the front seats of a Chevy Impala (thankfully, the car

was a convertible!). While it looks pretty hokey by today's standards, the commercial was a real conversation-starter when it first appeared.

Texaco

To get their share of the burgeoning automobile market in post-war America, gasoline brands fought aggressively for awareness and sales at the pump. Those were the days when gas station attendants actually came out to cars to pump gas, check the oil and wipe windshields. Texaco was one of the gasoline brands that most successfully leveraged television. The brand was already well-known as the sponsor of Texaco Star Theater, a comedy variety show that was broadcast on radio and made the move to television in 1948. Texaco Star Theater launched the television career of the show's host, comedian Milton Berle, who became affectionately known as "Uncle Miltie." The weekly evening program was so beloved (it was rated #1 in the 1950-51 season) that Texaco Star Theater is given credit for fueling the meteoric sales of television sets during that time. Although Texaco discontinued sponsoring the show in 1953, the brand's awareness was solidified. Texaco's TV commercials were also widely recognized because of the company's jingle, "You can trust your car to the man who wears the star... the big, bright Texaco star."

Beauty and Health

As consumers emerged from the self-sacrificing war years, they gained vitality and a verve for life. This led to a new emphasis on looking good and feeling good. Makers of beauty and health products were happy to oblige consumers with a bewildering array of choices. Women's cosmetics were heavily advertised, as were all kinds of personal beauty products. Over-the-counter medications also took advantage of television advertising.

Alka-Seltzer

Alka-Seltzer, a pain reliever and antacid tablet that fizzed when dropped into water, had its beginnings in 1931. It made use of print and radio advertising for promotion, along with sponsorships of radio programs. The real marketing breakthrough for Alka-Seltzer, though, came in 1951 with the creation of a little mascot called "Sparky" but quickly renamed "Speedy" in keeping with the product's promotional theme, "Speedy Relief." Speedy's smiling elfin face sat atop a body made out of an Alka-Seltzer tablet; he wore another tablet as his hat. Speedy also carried a little wand that he used as a pointer. While Speedy first appeared in magazine advertising, he was brilliantly brought to life in television commercials through animation. Appearing with comedian Buster Keaton in the earliest commercials, Speedy sang the jingle, "Relief is just a swallow away." Between 1954 and 1964, Speedy was used in over 200 Alka-Seltzer commercials. The popular munchkin reappeared in new commercials even into the 21st Century, singing another classic jingle, "Plop plop, fizz fizz, oh what a relief it is."

Burma-Shave

Burma-Shave, one of the original brushless shaving creams, first became nationally known for its unusual method of outdoor advertising. As early as 1925, the Burma-Vita Company promoted its Burma-Shave brand by placing a series of rhyming signs along roads. Typically, four or five signs would be placed one after the other, some distance apart, so they could be read by motorists. The first signs appeared just in Minnesota, where the company was located, but they were so successful in increasing sales that Burma-Shave signs began to appear across the country. At the height of their popularity in the 1950s, Burma-Shave signs were seen on mostly rural roads in 44 states. In one TV commercial, a woman narrates the signs as they appear on a road: "Within this vale/ Of toil and sin/ Your head grows bald/ But not your chin/ Burma Shave." The road signs were eliminated soon after 1963, when the company was sold to American Safety Razor (which later became Gillette).

Camay and Lifebuoy
Skin care was at the forefront of personal hygiene in post-war America. When it came to facial appearance, women's cosmetics were significant, but at the most basic level, soap brands were given a promotional boost in early television commercials. Most soaps pre-dated the television era, so they already had some brand awareness, but through television, soap brands could distinguish themselves. Camay, introduced by Procter & Gamble in 1926, was positioned as "the soap for beautiful women." Early television commercials boasted that Camay could give women a "clearer, fresher complexion. You'll see your skin come out of the shadows." Lifebuoy, (*Appendix, 27*) created by Lever Brothers in 1894, was the first soap to contain carbolic acid, a stringent, poisonous substance. It was fine for cleaning floors and washing clothes, but Lever Brothers turned Lifebuoy into a personal soap product by introducing a toilet bar in 1933. With all of the competitive soaps available for women in the 1950s, Lifebuoy broke the mold by targeting men. One 1950s

television commercial pitched "new mint refresher" Lifebuoy as "a soap so loaded with mint, so tangy, so frosty... it drives wives wicked."

Halo and Prell

Shampoo was a major beauty product category in the 1950s, and two brands that fought for market share were Halo and Prell. Halo, introduced in 1938 by Colgate-Palmolive, had the unique selling proposition of being "soap free." Claiming to contain no oils or harsh chemicals, Halo "glorified" hair and was sold with a double-your-money-back guarantee. Halo shampoo became familiar to consumers through its jingle, "Halo, Everybody, Halo," which was repeated on radio and in early television commercials by the likes of superstars Peggy Lee and Frank Sinatra. Procter & Gamble's Prell shampoo came out a decade later (1947); its positioning as a luxury shampoo was distinctly different from Halo. Early television commercials targeting women focused on the rich, luxurious feeling from shampooing with Prell. One very memorable commercial showed a pearl slowly sinking in a bottle of the thick green liquid.

Mum, Ban and Secret

Mum was the first deodorant, responsible for starting a major health category, deodorants and anti-perspirants. Invented in 1888 as a cream to be applied to the underarms, "Mum" (*Appendix, 28*) was the nickname of a nurse who helped the unknown inventor. Mum was advertised in a 1952 television commercial in which a female spy was shown delivering a message about the deodorant; she then speaks to her superior on the phone, using the product's slogan, "Mum's the word." Mum's real claim to fame, however, was the development of the first roll-on deodorant in the 1950s. It was marketed in the United States under the name Ban Roll-on. Ban was made into a spray in the 1960s. When Secret was introduced in 1956, Procter & Gamble put its marketing muscle into pitching it as the first deodorant/anti-perspirant created especially for women. Television commercials promoting Ice Blue Secret, the roll-on version, used the slogan, "cool...calm...dry."

Cereal

Cereal redefined breakfast for the American family of the 1950s; cold and later hot cereal flourished during the decade primarily because of its popularity with children. Boomer kids couldn't get enough of the sweet stuff and busy parents went along with it, sometimes begrudgingly. As indicated earlier, Cheerios was a leading World War II brand, but after the war, the cereal triumvirate (General Mills, Kellogg and Post) began producing an endless variety of cereal brands, many of which have lasted to this day... because who doesn't love cereal?

Cocoa Puffs (General Mills) and Cocoa Krispies (Kellogg's)

Cocoa Puffs and Cocoa Krispies exemplify the competition between the two leading cereal manufacturers. Both of these cereals were introduced in 1958 and, by the early 1960s, one was trying to outdo the other. Cocoa Puffs, a chocolate version of Kix cereal, promoted the fact that it contained Hershey's cocoa. A character named Sonny the Cuckoo Bird appeared on the box and as an animated cartoon character in early television commercials, exclaiming, "I'm coo-coo for Cocoa Puffs!" Cocoa

Krispies is a chocolate version of the 1927 cereal, Rice Krispies. Early Cocoa Krispies commercials featured different cartoon characters, including Snagglepuss the Lion (notably goofier than Tony the Tiger). Later, however, Kellogg's put Snap, Crackle and Pop – the three elves who promoted Rice Krispies – on the Cocoa Krispies box to more closely associate it with the Rice Krispies brand. You can still find Cocoa Puffs and Cocoa Krispies in the cereal aisle.

Frosted Flakes (Kellogg's)
First branded as "Sugar Frosted Flakes" in 1952, this iconic cereal wasn't renamed Frosted Flakes until the 1980s. The idea for Frosted Flakes was simple: Turn the company's flagship brand, Corn Flakes, into a kid-friendly sweetened version. A little-known fact is that Tony the Tiger had to compete with a kangaroo, an elephant and a gnu to win his position as the cereal's official mascot. The cartoon character Tony was introduced on the cereal package and in print ads right from the beginning. Kids were thrilled when Tony came to life as an animated cartoon tiger, jumping off the box in early TV commercials to proclaim that Sugar Frosted Flakes were "G-r-r-r-r-eat!" As with most cereals of the time, Sugar Frosted Flakes television commercials were directed to kids; one commercial even featured actor George Reeves, the star of the popular children's television show, Superman. Frosted Flakes continues as one of the world's most popular cereals. A more contemporary Tony the Tiger is its durable mascot.

Maypo

Consider Maypo an outlier in the great cereal wars, both because it was a hot cereal and it was the product of an obscure small company, Maltex. Still, it holds an important spot in cereal history: Maypo was the first maple flavored hot oatmeal cereal to be introduced in 1953 – a decade before Quaker Oats marketed instant oatmeal. Maypo had some tough work to do to get noticed, but it succeeded thanks to one 1956 animated television commercial. In it, a father attempts to get his son Marky to eat Maypo cereal but the boy refuses. Exasperated, the man tastes the cereal and finds that he likes it. That's when Marky realizes he's missing out on something good, so he yells, "I want my Maypo!" This beloved (if annoyingly exclaimed) slogan was turned into a series of commercials in which sports celebrities Mickey Mantle (baseball) and Johnny Unitas (football) appeared, proclaiming the very same thing.

Cigarettes

As mentioned previously, cigarette smoking gained popularity during World War II. However, in the early 1950s, there was increasing concern regarding the health risks of smoking, so cigarette sales started to decline. According to the March 1999 issue of the journal, *Tobacco Control*, tobacco companies met in late 1953 to discuss positive ways to market cigarettes. It turned out to be collusion: They reportedly all agreed to stop focusing on health claims of any kind. As a result, cigarette advertising after that time sought to differentiate cigarettes on the basis of such factors as flavor and lifestyle. Cigarette advertisers were among the heaviest users of television commercials until cigarette advertising was banned on television in 1971.

Kool and Newport

Kool, (*Appendix*, 29) a 1933 mentholated cigarette brand, was recognizable because of its mascot, a cute illustrated penguin character named Willie, who was printed on the package as well as on each cigarette. During the early television era, Willie was animated and spoke the word, "Kool." One television commercial integrated Willie with filmed images of a "snow fresh" stream. A woman's voice was heard singing, "Smoke Kool… Kool… Kool." A male smoker in the commercial suggests, "Why don't you switch from hot to the snow fresh coolness of Kool." Newport, another mentholated brand, wasn't launched until 1957. A color television commercial from the 1960s invoked a sense of playful fantasy when characters from the commercial were seen to "jump out" of the television screen and greet a male TV-watching consumer who lights up a Newport cigarette. Newport became the best-selling menthol brand by 1993.

Marlboro

It may be hard to believe, but Marlboro was originally positioned as a cigarette for women in the 1920s and 1930s; its slogan was "Mild as May," and a printed red band on each cigarette was supposed to hide a lady's lipstick stain. World War II came along and Marlboro sales fell, so tobacco company Philip Morris decided to reposition the brand as a man's cigarette. Early television commercials showed a male smoker while the jingle, "You get a lot to like with a Marlboro – filter, flavor, pack or box," was heard in the background. In 1954, along came one of the winningest concepts in cigarette advertising – the "Marlboro Man." The aspirational imagery showed a series of rugged looking men, the most popular of which was a cowboy who inhabited "Marlboro Country." The Marlboro Man became the central theme of an inspired television advertising campaign that employed the theme song from the 1960 Western movie, "The Magnificent Seven." The commercials are credited with turning the manly Marlboro brand into the leading cigarette sold since the early 1970s.

Winston

Celebrity endorsements of cigarettes were common in the 1950s; for example, Philip Morris cigarettes were promoted by Lucille Ball and Desi Arnaz in commercials and on their popular TV show, sponsored by the brand. Winston, introduced in 1954, also used celebrity endorsement and sponsorship, but the brand took a more novel approach. In 1960, an animated television series called The Flintstones was the first to appear in the primetime television slot. R. J. Reynolds, maker of the Winston brand, saw a unique opportunity to be associated with a cartoon show that had cross-generational appeal, so Winston sponsored The Flintstones through the 1962 season. Not only was the brand prominently featured within the show, the characters Barney and Fred also promoted the brand in animated commercials. In one spot, they lament the fact that their wives are working so hard; Barney suggests, "Let's go around back where we can't see 'em." That's when they light up their Winstons as Barney intones the cigarette's famous tag line, "Winston tastes good...like a cigarette should." It may or may not have been due to sponsorship of The Flintstones, but by 1966, Winston was the world's best-selling cigarette and remained at the top until it was knocked out of first place by Marlboro.

Cleansers and Detergents

Cleaning the house and washing the family's clothes were tasks relegated to the American housewife during the 1950s, so it's only natural that products in this category appeared during daytime television programs – "soap operas" as well as game and talk shows. While numerous cleansers and detergents were introduced at the time, the leading manufacturer by far was Procter & Gamble.

Ajax

Introduced in 1947 by Colgate-Palmolive, Ajax Powdered Cleanser was a bathroom cleaning product whose brand name was applied to a whole family of products in the 1960s – attesting to its staying power. An early TV commercial for Ajax featured several animated "cleansing elves" using the product in a bathroom and singing a jingle about "Ajax (bum bum) the foaming cleanser." The slogan, "Stronger than dirt," was also prominently featured in advertising for Ajax Powdered Cleanser and later for Ajax Laundry Detergent.

Ivory Snow

Ivory was Procter & Gamble's first soap product, introduced as bar soap in 1879. Ivory Flakes, a powder version of the soap, was popular in the 1920s as a snow substitute for home Christmas trees and decorations. The dish washing version of Ivory soap, Ivory Snow, borrowed the soap's claim of being "99 44/100% pure." An early television commercial showed a housewife using Ivory Snow, saying it's the "safest possible soap you can buy for your hands in the dishpan... and it's granulated for speedy suds..." Since only the wealthiest families had automatic dishwashers in the 1950s, dish washing products like Ivory Snow were important household products for washing dishes by hand.

Mr. Clean

This eponymous all-purpose cleaner, another Procter & Gamble product, was actually purchased by the company in 1958 and introduced to consumers the same year. A remarkably versatile cleaning liquid, Mr. Clean quickly gained popularity and became the leading household cleaner in less than one year because it could clean virtually anything around the house – even the family dog. There was something else lovable about Mr. Clean – namely "Mr. Clean" himself, a muscular, bald-headed masculine but subservient character with an earring (very daring for his day). Perhaps he also fulfilled some housewives' subliminal fantasies! An early television commercial depicted consumers using the product, accompanied by an animated version of Mr. Clean and the memorable jingle, "Mr. Clean gets rid of dirt and grime and grease in just a minute, Mr. Clean will clean your whole house and everything that's in it... Mr. Clean, Mr. Clean, Mr. Clean!" An updated Mr. Clean character is featured on the product still sold today.

Tide

Only three years after Tide laundry detergent was introduced in 1946, it became the leading detergent brand in the United States. It was certainly helped along by the top loading washing machines that so many middle-class families bought in the 1950s – because a box of Tide was conveniently packaged with every new machine! An early television commercial proclaims that Tide is "the cleanest clean under the sun," as an attentive mom uses a fluffy clean towel to wrap up her child, who has just scampered out of the ocean onto a sandy beach. From the 1950s onward, Tide has been one of Procter & Gamble's major brands, spawning a whole host of brand extensions and innovations to keep the product relevant and thriving.

Convenience Foods

Advances in kitchen appliances and food production were an integral part of modern American life in the 1950s – so much so that there was a fundamental shift in cooking methods and food consumption by American families. Canned goods, which had been scarce during World War II, returned to well-stocked supermarket shelves. Innovations in frozen foods combined with improved refrigeration technology to create a dramatic increase in the frozen food section. Cookbooks featuring simple recipes were wildly popular at the time – especially the Betty Crocker Cookbook, first published in 1950. Processed foods were a boon to busy housewives; while the nutritional value of packaged food may have been suspect, American women sure loved the convenience of being able to prepare quick and easy meals for their families.

Birds Eye and Green Giant

Clarence Birdseye created a method for flash freezing food in 1924, based on his observations of the way the Inuit flash froze fish in Newfoundland. He invented and patented a "Quick Freeze Machine" that revolutionized frozen food processing. General Foods purchased Birdseye's company in 1929 and introduced the Birds Eye brand in 1930 in a limited market test of less than twenty stores in one state. The products were so well received that by the 1950s, Birds Eye was an international frozen foods leader. One 1950s TV commercial featured frozen concentrated orange juice with three animated children singing "Better Buy Birds Eye." Green Giant began as the Minnesota Valley Canning Company in 1903, but the Green Giant brand itself became so popular that the company was renamed Green Giant Company in 1950. The 1925 introduction of a canned product, "Green Giant Great Big Tender Peas," was followed three years later by the Green Giant character. He was first animated using stop-motion in an early TV commercial but didn't look very friendly, so in the 1960s, he was recast as an animated Green Giant with happy little helpers working "in the valley of the Jolly (Ho Ho Ho) Green Giant."

JELL-O

JELL-O (*Appendix, 30*) gelatin was already popular at the turn of the 20th Century – so how did it re-emerge as a favorite food of the Fifties? Housewives of the 1950s and 1960s were intrigued by cookbooks that depicted "salads" taking advantage of JELL-O's gelatinous ability to hold other ingredients together in a weird kind of suspended animation. The JELL-O salad craze even pervaded elegant dinner parties, during which elaborate molded creations containing pieces of vegetables or fruit were served. JELL-O didn't stop there – the brand was also extended to include instant puddings, which kids loved all by themselves or as pie fillings. A 1950s television commercial featured Roy Rogers speaking directly to children, telling them how easy it was to make up some JELL-O Instant Pudding for dessert. At the end of the spot, Roy is accompanied by Dale Evans and a group of kids in a lively rendition of the JELL-O Instant Pudding song.

Kraft Singles, Cheez Whiz and Velveeta

Kraft redefined cheese with a line of cheesy products that were popular in the 1950s. Kraft Singles, introduced in 1949, is emblematic of processed food; in fact, it was called a "processed cheese food" rather than "cheese." No matter, moms appreciated the convenience – and kids loved Kraft Singles slapped between two slices of white bread to make yummy grilled cheese sandwiches. Cheez Whiz, marketed by Kraft first in the United Kingdom and then in the United States in 1953, was a cheese sauce that could be used on any food; it was especially good and gooey on nachos and hot dogs. Velveeta, a processed cheese product that could be sliced and melted easily, was acquired by Kraft in 1927. It achieved a loyal following during the 1950s when it was turned into a cheese spread. Today, the Velveeta product family is formidable, with more than fifty different Velveeta-based foods. Kraft employed a TV series, Kraft Television Theatre, along with television commercials, to promote its cheese products. Kraft Television Theatre began in 1947 and ran for over ten years, during which time it aired hundreds of dramas and comedies.

Nestlé's Quik and Ovaltine

In the 1950s, milk was thought to be important for children's developing bones and growing bodies – but most kids didn't like drinking milk – they only tolerated it in cereal. To make milk more pleasing to a child's palate, a variety of milk additives were invented, among them Bosco, Hershey's Syrup, ill-fated

Flav-R-Straws and two powdered substances, Nestlé's Quik and Ovaltine. Ovaltine (*Appendix, 31*) was invented in Switzerland in the early 1900s, but it became popular in the United States when it sponsored the Little Orphan Annie and Captain Midnight radio shows, and then the Captain Midnight children's television series in the mid 1950s. That's when kids were asked to send in proofs of Ovaltine purchase in order to receive a "secret decoder ring." An absurd 1955 Ovaltine commercial featuring Captain Midnight (Richard Webb) shows children in adult roles – flying a jet plane, captaining a ship and driving an ambulance! Nestlé, a Swiss company, introduced Nestlé's Quik to the U.S. market in 1948, shortening the name to Nesquik for the European market. Decades later, the product was renamed Nesquik globally. TV commercials in the mid 1950s featured ventriloquist Jimmy Nelson with two puppets, a boy (Dan) and a dog (Farfel). The duo always sang the memorable jingle: "N-e-s-t-l-e-s, Nestlé's makes the very best...chocolate!"

Swanson TV Dinner
The 1954 "Swanson TV Brand Frozen Dinner" is credited with starting prepackaged meals, a frozen foods category that took the decade by storm. After all, didn't every family want to eat dinner in front of the television? I recounted the story of this legendary innovation in my book, *BOOMER BRANDS*:

> The mother of invention for this product was a turkey – actually 260 tons of turkey that Swanson & Sons was stuck with, surely the world's record for Thanksgiving leftovers. What to do, what to do? Gerry Thomas, a Swanson salesman, found inspiration in airline food trays, and tons of turkey were turned into trays of ready-made turkey

dinners. Swanson sold ten million of these all-in-one meals in the first year. They switched to paper trays when the microwave oven became a consumer favorite – but by then, Swanson had started a whole class of ready-made meals that remains popular in the frozen foods section of today's grocery stores.

Swanson advertised its frozen dinners with early commercials that focused on the convenience of the dinners for moms and the tag line, "You can trust Swanson." Frozen prepared meals have been an American staple ever since Swanson's breakthrough product was invented.

Fashion

Women were interested in both practical and glamorous fashion in the 1950s. Moving away from the war's understated, frugal fashions, Christian Dior created what became known as the "new look" – a style that called attention to a woman's hourglass figure and made ample use of fabric. Still, women embraced with equal enthusiasm casual sportswear, including sundresses and felt, circular skirts that became known as "poodle skirts" for the dogs and other lighthearted designs that appeared on them. Men's fashion veered from business suits for the older set to James Dean-inspired t-shirts and jeans for young bucks.

Hush Puppies

Hush Puppies started something of a craze when they were introduced in 1958. Unlike stiff leather black or brown dress shoes of the time, Hush Puppies were made from soft suede that could be dyed in numerous colors. They came in several styles and were the first real casual shoe for women, men and children. During the era, tired feet were known as "barking dogs," and "hush puppies" were fried corn fritters made on farms that were often thrown to dogs to keep them quiet, so the shoes were named accordingly. Hush Puppies further enhanced the brand name by choosing an adorable basset hound as the brand mascot. The shoes were heavily advertised in print and on television during their introduction. They eventually became so popular that they graced the feet of ordinary folks as well as such celebrities as Frank Sinatra and The Beatles. Hush Puppies had a revival in the mid-90s thanks to fashion designers who brought the retro style back.

Maidenform and Playtex
Women's undergarments came to the surface in both magazine advertising and television commercials during the 1950s. Two of the best-known brands, Maidenform and Playtex, engaged in the battle of the bras. Beginning in 1949, Maidenform, at the time the market leader, primarily used magazine ads to execute their "I dreamed..." campaign, a daring and some would say racy series of ads. Each ad pictured a woman wearing just a Maidenform bra and nothing else on top, along with other clothing on bottom. For example, in an ad with the headline, "I dreamed I went on a safari in my Maidenform bra," the woman was wearing the bra along with zebra-patterned safari pants. Provocative for its time, the series included over 160 variations on the theme and ran for twenty years. Playtex, on the other hand, promoted its "cross your heart" bra in a much tamer manner. An early television commercial showed a number of women whispering, "You're suddenly shapelier..." to each other.

One of them finishes the thought, saying "...in a Playtex Cross-Your-Heart Bra." Playtex continued to lag behind Maidenform in sales until the mid 1960s, when it substantially gained market share.

Timex
Timex watches became legitimate fashion accessories for both women and men in the 1950s. After Waterbury Clock Company assisted the United States in World War II by manufacturing precision timers, the firm changed its name to United States Time Corporation. The Timex brand, introduced by the company in 1950, was the first watch to incorporate a high quality mass-produced watch movement, making it reliable as well as affordable. Timex achieved breakthrough awareness in 1958 with a series of weekly commercials in which TV personality John Cameron Swayze punished a Timex watch, live on television. In each commercial, he repeated the slogan, "Takes a licking and keeps on ticking." In one commercial, Swayze attached a ladies' Timex to a dishwasher with a glass door, ran it for a while, took the watch out and held it to a microphone so viewers could hear that it was still ticking. Live television didn't always cooperate, though; one time, Swayze attached a Timex watch to an outboard motor in a special glass tub and it fell off before he could prove it was still working. But the commercials were timely: By the end of the decade, one out of every three watches sold in the U.S. was a Timex.

Music
American music was undergoing a major transformation in the late 1940s and 1950s. The Big Band/Swing sound of the 1940s

was replaced by strong vocalists with backup bands who emerged late in the decade and into the 1950s. Soon, singers became personal brands of their own; stars such as Tony Bennett, Frankie Laine, Patti Page and Frank Sinatra were living legends. Later in the decade, popular music transitioned to doo wop and rock 'n' roll, when such stars as Chuck Berry, Jerry Lee Lewis and Elvis Presley achieved fame. Many musical personalities raised their brand awareness by appearing on the Ed Sullivan Show and after 1957, on American Bandstand.

Chuck Berry

Chuck Berry is acknowledged by most pop musicologists as one of the most influential rock 'n' rollers. In 1955, his recording of "Maybellene" topped the rhythm and blues chart, selling over one million copies. Berry wrote and recorded numerous rock classics, including "Johnny B. Goode, "Roll Over Beethoven" and "Sweet Little Sixteen." Many of his songs were covered by other recording stars. Berry was himself a major star by the end of the decade, with hit records, appearances in films and a featured spot in 1958 on The Dick Clark Show, a weekly evening television program that showcased America's top pop talent. The Beatles openly credited Berry for inspiring many of their early songs.

Elvis Presley

If any one individual typified pop stardom, it was the man who was internationally known by his first name, Elvis. The Tennessee native started out as a regional rock singer in the mid 1950s but hit it big nationally with the release of "Heartbreak Hotel" in 1956 which became a number one record. From then on, Elvis cemented his reputation as the "King of Rock 'n' Roll," recording multiple hits and starring in motion pictures, interrupted only by two years of military service from 1958 to 1960. Elvis was also a major television personality, appearing on national television shows such as the Ed Sullivan Show and his own televised " '68 Comeback Special." Elvis Presley, who died at age 42 in 1977, continues to hold the position of best-selling solo artist of all time.

Frank Sinatra
Frank Sinatra was arguably one of the great personal brands of post-war America. He gained popularity as a swing era singer as early as the mid 1940s. His fame blossomed when, in the 1950s, he began a long series of Las Vegas performances. Sinatra's Academy Award-winning role in the 1953 film, *From Here to Eternity*, was the start of a very successful motion picture career that overlapped with an equally impressive recording career. He also had his own radio program and two iterations of a television program, The Frank Sinatra Show, which ran from 1950 – 1952 and 1957 – 1958. Sinatra's other claim to fame, which served to further boost his personal profile, was his leading role in a group of performers known as the "Rat Pack." Sinatra, Dean Martin, Sammy Davis, Jr., Joey Bishop and Peter Lawford (who later left) took Las Vegas by storm and appeared together in movies in the early 1960s.

Snack Foods
Snack foods have been a popular (and unfortunate) part of the American diet for over one hundred years. In 1900, the Hershey chocolate bar was invented, in 1912, the Oreo cookie was intro-

duced and in 1914, Tastykakes were created. The Twenties was the candy era – Baby Ruth, Butterfinger, Milky Way, Oh Henry! and Reese's Peanut Butter Cups all debuted. The 1930s weren't too shabby, either – that decade produced Fritos, Lay's, Snickers, Tootsie Rolls and Twinkies. The 1940s gave birth to Almond Joy, Cheetos, Junior Mints, M&Ms and Whoppers. In the 1950s and 1960s, television was an ideal promotional vehicle for snack food producers, who largely targeted children in much the same way as cereal makers did. Snack foods back then were also distinguished by a new emphasis on packaging. Bags, boxes, tins and other bright, bold snack food containers were ingeniously designed to have kid appeal.

Drake's
Drake's began as Newman Drake's bakery in New York in 1896. Two of the favorite Drake snack cakes of the Fifties – Devil Dogs and Yankee Doodles – were actually created in the Twenties. Others, such as Ring Dings, Funny Bones and Yodels, were produced in the 1950s and 1960s, when Drake's catered to a burgeoning demographic, Boomer kids. (Parents may not have admitted it, but they liked the occasional snack cake, too.) An early Drake's TV commercial for Yodels shows two young boys talking about "yodeling," which of course meant eating Yodels. At the end of the commercial, an animated duck (the same one that appeared on Drake's packaging) encouraged kids to head to the store and pick up a package of Yodels. Drake's archrival, Hostess, was also churning out kid-oriented goodies at the time, including Ding Dongs, Ho Hos, Sno Balls and the beloved Boomer favorite, Twinkies.

E-Z Pop and Jiffy Pop

Before microwave popcorn, there was the cleverly designed tin pan containing popcorn and oil that kids (with parental supervision) could pop right on the stove. It was especially cool to watch the bright silver tin foil expand during the popping process. Two competitors fought it out for market share. E-Z Pop was the first to introduce the idea in 1954. It was accompanied by a quirky animated commercial featuring two pieces of popcorn, a "father" and "son," reciting a kind of beatnik talking jazz song about E-Z Pop. Five years later, Jiffy Pop debuted. An early commercial depicted two kids with a genie who demonstrated the product and claimed, "Jiffy Pop, Jiffy Pop, the magic treat, as much fun to make as it is to eat." When Jiffy Pop became more POPular, the maker of E-Z Pop sued. E-Z Pop won, but the case was overturned on appeal. As a result, Jiffy Pop went on to out-pop the original, so E-Z Pop flopped. Despite microwave popcorn, Jiffy Pop remains on the market.

PEZ

PEZ was an innovative candy/candy dispenser combination that came to the United States in the 1950s. It's a little-known fact that PEZ was actually created in 1927 by Austrian Eduard Haas III to help cigarette smokers break the habit. At the time, PEZ candies were only made in peppermint flavor and dispensed from a contraption similar in size and shape to a lighter. In the United States, the candy flavors were expanded and the "lighter" was ingeniously reconfigured to add the heads of kid-friendly characters to the top. As a result, kids could pop a PEZ from the "mouths" of Mickey Mouse, Batman and scores of other fictional favorites into their own mouths. Early marketing for PEZ was innovative, too: One of the earliest TV commercials offered a free PEZ "Cocoa Martian" dispenser and candy refill with the purchase of Cocoa Marsh, a milk additive. The dispenser and candy were attached to Cocoa Marsh jars, making it an irresistible promotional tag-along. The "candy with character" grew in popularity in subsequent decades. Today, Americans consume billions of PEZ candies each year and the confection is sold in more than 90 countries.

Soft Drinks

In post-war America, soft drinks were the liquid equivalent of cereal. Soft drinks were just as sickeningly sweet, high carb and nutritiously empty as most cereals of the era, but that didn't thwart their popularity with kids and adults alike. Coca-Cola had already become America's favorite cola, enhanced by its wartime prominence, while Pepsi-Cola was a strong second. The cola wars were further intensified by a popular competitor in the Fifties, RC Cola. Other soft drinks – sodas as well as the non-carbonated variety, such as Kool-Aid and Tang – kept Americans imbibing sweet stuff, whether it was from soda fountains, bottles or aluminum cans, which were introduced in 1957.

Diet Rite and RC Cola

Royal Crown Cola, later known as RC Cola, derived from a dispute over the distribution of Coca-Cola syrup in the early 1900s. In the 1950s, Royal Crown Cola may have lagged behind Coca-Cola and Pepsi-Cola in market share, but in some ways it was more innovative. Royal Crown sodas were the first to be sold in cans. In 1958, Royal Crown introduced the first diet cola,

Diet Rite. Unfortunately, it was sweetened with cyclamate and saccharin, the first of which was eventually deemed dangerous to humans. Still, Diet Rite forged the way for other brands to later launch sugar-free soft drinks. RC heavily advertised on television in the 1960s and 1970s. One campaign featured puppets created by Jim Henson; another TV commercial starred Nancy Sinatra singing about the brand.

Kool-Aid
While Kool-Aid originated in the 1920s, the brand took advantage of the convenience foods revolution when it was sold to a major food manufacturer, General Foods, in 1953. Marketed as a powdered drink, Kool-Aid became a favorite of kids when the animated "Kool-Aid Man," a pitcher of Kool-Aid stylized with a human face, first appeared on TV screens in the 1950s. One early commercial showed a mom and her kids singing along with the Kool-Aid Man and enjoying the drink. Mom says, "...a 5-cent package makes two full quarts." The kids chime in, "...for the very best drink you ever made," followed by the Kool-Aid Man singing, "...be sure that the envelope says Kool-Aid." Kool-Aid remains an enduring brand, which today includes a line of powders, liquids and juice packets.

Nesbitt's Orange
Nesbitt's Orange, a bottled soda with 10 percent California orange juice, was a pre-war favorite when it was introduced in 1938. It continued to gain market share and became the best-selling orange soda during the late 1940s and 1950s. On the back of its bottles appeared the slogan, "Nesbitt's name on a soft drink is like STERLING stamped on silver." In 1946, Nesbitt's

print advertising featured Marilyn Monroe, an obscure model who would later become a top Hollywood starlet. Among its marketing innovations was the brand's sponsorship of a very early California children's television puppet show, Ricky and the Magic Trolley. Nesbitt's Orange scored a marketing coup when it was named the "Official Orange Drink" of Disneyland from its opening in 1955 into the 1960s. The drink was said to be a favorite of Elvis Presley. The Nesbitt's Orange brand was ultimately overtaken by such competitors as Orange Crush and Fanta Orange soda.

Toothpaste

Whiter teeth, fresher breath and a reduction in cavities were all important when it came to caring for teeth in the 1950s. Dental disease, in fact, was a major problem in the U.S. in the early 1940s, when Americans were afflicted with some 700 million cavities annually. At the time, toothpastes were designed primarily for cosmetic purposes, not to prevent cavities. That changed in the 1950s, when numerous toothpaste brands, each with its own unique marketing pitch emphasizing health benefits, competed for market share in a hotly contested product category.

Crest

Procter & Gamble was the first to test a new toothpaste containing fluoride in 1955 – Crest with "Fluoristan." Research showed that Crest resulted in a definitive reduction in cavities among both children and adults, so the company rolled out the product nationwide in 1956. The American Dental Association was impressed enough to offer its endorsement to Crest in

1960; two years later, Crest had become the nation's best-selling toothpaste. The brand's early advertising, both in print and on television, featured a happy girl exclaiming to her mother, "Look mom, no cavities!" Since the early 1960s, Crest has flourished and grown into one of P&G's leading brands, with product extensions beyond toothpaste alone.

Ipana

The Ipana (*Appendix, 32*) toothpaste brand existed long before Crest – it was introduced by Bristol-Myers as early as 1901. But with competition from Crest, Bristol-Myers needed to differentiate Ipana. In 1954, the company pinned its hopes on Disney, who created a cartoon mascot for Ipana named "Bucky Beaver." Animated by Disney and voiced by head Mouseketeer Jimmie Dodd, Bucky sang and danced on behalf of Ipana in television commercials. Bucky also appeared in comic strip ads. Ipana remained a popular, competitive toothpaste brand through the 1960s. However, Bristol-Myers saw more business opportunities in the pharmaceuticals market and paid less attention to the brand; by the 1970s, Ipana was gone. But Bucky and Ipana may make a return to the toothpaste category, because a company has shown interest in bringing it back as a retro brand.

Pepsodent

Like Ipana, Pepsodent, (*Appendix, 33*) marketed in the United States since 1915, pre-dated Crest. Pepsodent sponsored Bob Hope's radio show from 1938 to 1948. In 1944, the brand was acquired by Unilever, a global marketer who was able to increase sales of Pepsodent dramatically in the United Kingdom. In the United States, however, Pepsodent's tardiness in adding fluoride to its formula caused it to lag behind Crest. The product claimed instead that it contained "Irium," which was found to be a meaningless term that simply represented one of Pepsodent's cleaning ingredients. Pepsodent became best known for the catchy jingle featured in its television commercials, "You'll wonder where the yellow went, when you brush your teeth with Pepsodent." While Pepsodent still exists, it is a minor brand sold primarily in discount stores.

Toys and Games

Radio, records and television were entertaining distractions for adults and children alike in post-war America, but there was no shortage of toys and games to occupy kids. The baby boom presented such toy and game manufacturers as Fisher-Price, Hasbro, Mattel, Milton Bradley, Parker Brothers and Wham-O with an unprecedented opportunity to market fun to youth. The toy market accommodated indoor and outdoor play, often separating toys by their appeal to either boys or girls as well as by age groups. Games were designed either for children to play independently or for the whole family to play together.

Barbie and Chatty Cathy

Dolls have been a perennial favorite of American girls. In 1959, Mattel created two of the most consequential doll brands: Barbie and Chatty Cathy. Both of these dolls were the brainchild of Ruth Handler. Barbie, named after Ruth's daughter Barbara, was a doll with an extensive fashion wardrobe, sold separately. She was joined in 1961 by Ken, named after Ruth's son Kenneth. Chatty Cathy was a unique doll that seemed to talk; a ring could be pulled and the doll would respond by speaking one of eleven phrases, such as "I love you." Seven more phrases were added in 1963. The technology behind Chatty Cathy was pretty simple – the ring was attached to a string that activated a tiny record player inside the doll. This same mechanism was used to produce an entire line of Mattel talking dolls. Television commercials promoted Barbie and Chatty Cathy separately. The first Barbie commercial featured the doll appearing with several outfits. The jingle ended with the lyric, "I'll make believe that I am you" – an aspirational statement relating the doll to every little girl watching the commercial. Chatty Cathy commercials focused on her ability to "speak" and also highlighted her outfits. As an aside, the phrase "chatty Cathy" came to mean someone who talks too much. Some 350,000 Barbie dolls were sold in the first year alone, and Barbie went on to become Mattel's largest, most profitable line of dolls and accessories. Barbie and Chatty Cathy were the two most popular dolls of the 1960s.

Candy Land

In 1949, right on the cusp of the 1950s, game company Milton Bradley introduced a new game called Candy Land. It was the creation of Eleanor Abbott, a woman afflicted with polio. She invented it for children who also contracted the disease. The game was unique because it was designed for preschool children too young to read. Instead of words, Candy Land featured colors on cards that matched up with colored squares on the game board. By picking the cards, kids could move playing pieces along a path that led them through various fanciful places, such as "Gumdrop Mountain" and "Peppermint Stick Forest," until they reached "Candy Castle." In an early television commercial, a man dressed as a police officer shows two very young children how to play the game. This classic game, still being made today, was the forerunner of many other games for children.

Frisbee and Hula Hoop

Some of the most successful toys of the 1950s were considered fads – wildly popular items that created a craze for a relatively short period of time. Two of those toys – the Frisbee and the Hula Hoop – were introduced to American kids by Wham-O, a California company. Wham-O got its name from the sound ("wham") made by its first toy, a slingshot, when the projectile from the slingshot hit a target. The Frisbee was derived from pie tins produced by the Frisbie Pie Company in Connecticut in the late 1800s. Just for fun, university students would throw the tins (without the pies), yelling "Frisbie!" The tin was refined into a plastic disc and sold to Wham-O who first named it the Pluto Platter and then changed its name to Frisbee. Early TV commercials showed kids playing a game of Frisbee. While the original Frisbee has remained popular, there have been scores of competitors who've produced similar flying discs. The Hula Hoop was not "new" when it was introduced by Wham-O in 1958. The fact is, people were dancing with hoops for thousands of years; in the United States, for example, Native Americans were known for their generations-old Hoop Dance. But from the point of view of a Boomer kid, the plastic, colorful Hula Hoop was a novelty that caused quite the sensation. A 1960s TV commercial pitched a "Shoop Shoop Hula Hoop" that made a sound. In less than four months, some 25 million Hula Hoops were sold, with more than 100 million sold in the first two years.

Trains

Toy trains, beloved by children for hundreds of years, were largely replaced by the more sophisticated electric model railroads in the 1950s. Boys and girls were thrilled to watch pint-sized locomotives pulling multiple cars and a caboose around tiny tracks that were often set among miniature villages. The realistic, meticulously detailed toy trains could chug, whistle and even blow "smoke," thanks to special pellets or oil dropped into the locomotive's heating element-equipped smokestack. The most popular Lionel model train was the 1948 Santa Fe F3. Lionel's scale model trains were prized by children as well as train collectors. Lionel was the dominant electric train brand of the time, with as much as $25 million in annual train sales in the 1950s. A 1962 television commercial was itself iconic: It depicted a boy and girl opening a gift of a Lionel train set in front of the tree on Christmas morning. A competing brand, American Flyer, was purchased by Lionel in 1967 in an effort to keep the electric train market alive; however, toys took a turn toward space as the Sixties progressed, so interest in trains declined. Lionel published its last train catalog in 1969.

• CHAPTER 10 •

The Modern Brand is Born

Economic growth, product proliferation and television converged in the crucible of post-war America to create the fertile soil needed for modern brands to take root and bloom. New products, many of them innovative, flooded the marketplace in virtually every category. Pent-up demand for goods and services drove consumer purchasing behavior. Americans enthusiastically embraced their role as materialistic mid-century consumers.

Brand marketers were quick to capitalize on the percolating American economy and competition among brands was intense. Makers of branded products wanted to get their piece of the consumer pie. Products had to be of decent quality and value to compete. Brand marketers had to understand not just their brands' competitive advantages, but how to secure brand preference from consumers who had many choices. Marketers began to study what drove purchase behavior and analyzed consumer demographics; age, race, gender, income, education and other characteristics were all significant in developing a profile of the target buyer.

Brand management was a strategy that took hold during the era. The practice of brand management was pioneered by Procter & Gamble. It originated in 1931, the brainchild of a young ad man, Neil McElroy, who was employed by the company. McElroy was working on an ad campaign for Camay, a brand of soap. McElroy recognized that Camay faced competition not just from other companies' products but from inside with P&G's own Ivory soap brand. According to Thomas K. McCraw, author of the book, *American Business 1920 – 2000: How It Worked*:

> In a now-famous memo, [McElroy] argued that more concentrated attention should be paid to Camay, and by extension to other P&G brands as well. In addition to having a person in charge of each brand, there should be a substantial team of people devoted to thinking about every aspect of marketing it. This dedicated group should attend to one brand and it alone. ... The concern of these managers would be the brand, which would be marketed as if it were a separate business. In this way the qualities of every brand would be distinguished from those of every other.

McElroy went on to become president of P&G in 1948 and, perhaps oddly, the country's Secretary of Defense in 1957 under President Eisenhower.

At P&G, brand management has been responsible for the proliferation of a remarkable portfolio of brands, beginning in the 1950s and up through the present day. Adhering to the brand management discipline, P&G has spawned many brands dominating their respective product categories, some of which have become billion-dollar global brands. Procter & Gamble reported net sales of over $70 billion in their 2020 Annual Report with 47 percent of sales in the United States, Canada and Puerto Rico. One-third of sales were in the "Fabric & Home Care" business segment. Acknowledging Procter & Gamble's success in marketing consumer products, the advertising industry widely adopted brand management.

Another key marketing principle that emerged during the early television era was known as the **Unique Selling Proposition (USP).** The USP was developed by creative ad man Rosser Reeves, co-founder of the advertising agency, Ted Bates & Co. According to Reeves, every product had to have a single differentiating and compelling reason for it to be purchased by consumers – otherwise it wasn't worthy of advertising support. Often, the USP was best expressed in a memorable advertising slogan; Reeves was known for writing or directing dozens of them, including "They melt in your mouth, not in your hand" (M&Ms) and "Fast, fast, fast relief" (Anacin). Reeves, who made innovative use of television advertising, believed in presenting products honestly and focusing on rational, claim-based sales arguments. He believed that advertising alone, no matter how effective, could not "save" an inferior product. As with brand management, the USP concept was soon adopted by other brand marketers and their advertising agencies.

Brand marketing was widely recognized in the 1950s as necessary to a brand's success, but the methods used to advertise brands were sometimes questioned. One of the more public indictments of advertising came in the form of social critic Vance Packard's 1957 book, *The Hidden Persuaders*. In his book, Packard exposes marketing elements, including motivational research and subliminal tactics, that he believed demonstrated the ways in which advertisers manipulated the public and created inducements for product purchase. Even though the book was largely criticized by the advertising industry, it was popular with consumers. Consumers were becoming more discerning about brand advertising.

Brand advertising was scorned by some consumers for another reason: Social norms of the time caused an apparent insensitivity by advertisers to certain groups. One of them was women. Many of the advertising messages that appeared in the 1950s and early 1960s were downright sexist and highly offensive to women. Products pitched to women centered around keeping clean houses, doing the laundry and dishes, and being attractive to men. It was fairly common for advertisers to address women in a disparaging tone when it came to taking care of their hair, their face, their hands, their bodies or the way they dressed so their husbands would be happy with their appearance. That approach was relatively harmless compared to the truly repugnant advertising promoting the supreme dominance of men. Here are just two examples:
- In 1952, a striking (literally) magazine ad for Chase & Sanborn Coffee showed a photograph of a man sitting on a chair with his hand raised, ready to spank a grown

woman over his knees. The ad's headline read, "If your husband ever finds out you're not 'store-testing' for fresher coffee…"

- In 1953, Alcoa Aluminum introduced new twist-open caps on catsup bottles headlining a magazine ad, "You mean a <u>woman</u> can open it?" The copy read that the cap could be opened "without a knife blade, a bottle opener, or even a husband."

Another openly denigrated group was African Americans. Offensive and insulting images of Blacks had been used in American advertising for decades, but it was no less evident in the 1950s. At the time, many companies advertising to white consumers either ignored the Black consumer completely or utilized Blacks in subservient or derogatory roles. Here is one particularly egregious example:

- A 1952 ad for Van Heusen shirts carried the headline, "4 out of 5 men want Oxfords… in these new Van Heusen styles." The accompanying illustration showed four smiling white men in shirts and ties. The fifth man was an angry-looking Black native with a naked torso, a bone in his hair, a ring through his nose and a necklace made from large teeth around his neck. A caption under the native read, "Rumor has it that even he would gladly swap his boar's teeth for a Van Heusen Oxford!"

Thankfully, some advertisers, such as Pepsi-Cola, were far more enlightened when it came to race. As early as 1940, Pepsi-Cola hired a Black salesman and in 1947, the company developed a program to target African Americans. A team led by Edward

Boyd, who previously worked for the National Urban League, was charged with promoting the soft drink to Black communities. Under Boyd's direction, Pepsi-Cola implemented some of the first advertising campaigns spotlighting African Americans, including "Leaders in their fields," a series of magazine ads that featured such prominent Blacks as Ralph Bunche and Gordon Parks. Even so, Pepsi-Cola abandoned the program by 1950. It was only after the Civil Rights Movement of the 1960s that the company once again targeted the African American consumer.

At the same time, there was an increasing awareness of the role of the Black consumer in society, at least on the part of Black marketers. Ebony and Jet, two magazines targeting the Black consumer, began publishing in 1945 and 1951 respectively. The first Black-owned advertising agency in America, the Chicago-based Cullers Agency, was founded in 1956.

The Creative Revolution of the 1960s

Advertising in the 1960s was brought to life in the popular television series, "Mad Men," featuring the egotistical protagonist, creative ad man Don Draper. The show opened a window into the inner workings of advertising agencies of the time. According to an April 3, 2015 article in *The New York Times*, "It was an era marked by the dominance of the creative executive, embodied by Draper; the formation of advertising conglomerates; the rise of television; the slow beginnings of increased opportunities for women and minorities; and the advent of innovative technologies, like the copy machine and the computer."

By the 1960s, advertising was transitioning from promoting brands with a hard sell – like a salesman concentrating on product features – to a soft sell – oriented toward a brand's unique appeal and the role it played in the consumer's lifestyle. Advertising agencies enhanced rational messaging by adding emotion to the mix; brands tried to pull at the heartstrings as well as the purse strings. The positioning of brands themselves was changing as well: Now brands weren't simply viewed as products – they had *personalities.*

Brand advertising took on a fresh veneer: It began to reflect the youthful America led by the vibrant young president, John F. Kennedy, who was elected in 1960. Increasingly, brand advertising was designed to sync up with the growing influence of the youth culture. Later, brand marketers began to acknowledge that America was going through transitional upheaval evidenced by various social movements, including anti-war, civil rights, gay rights and women's liberation. The result was a full blown "creative revolution" emphasizing ads that were clever, bold and brash – and sometimes unconventional and iconoclastic. Television advertising played a key role, allowing even more creativity with the advent of color television.

Several classic brand marketing campaigns during the decade foretold the emergence of the modern American brand. Here are just a few examples:

- The "Marlboro Man" campaign, referenced earlier, started in 1954. It utilized outdoor imagery focusing on rugged, attractive men (especially cowboys) who inhabited "Marlboro Country," a mythical place that had the open expanse of the American West. The campaign integrated print advertising, billboards and television commercials that used the theme song from the 1960 Western movie, "The Magnificent Seven." In 1971, when Philip Morris wanted to market Marlboro to Black consumers, the company came up with what they thought was a simple solution: Take the white cowboy and turn him into a Black cowboy. Luckily, before they finalized the idea, they conferred with Tom Burrell, a Black ad man. He recommended instead that the Marlboro Man be transformed into a figure the Black consumer could relate to, namely a cool, urban, cigarette smoking Black dude. It worked – and Burrell was soon applying the same strategy to major brands in other categories. Marlboro became the leading cigarette brand, thanks in large part to the original Marlboro Man and his Black counterpart. The Marlboro Man was resilient, too – he lasted in U.S. advertising until 1999. The campaign went far beyond advertising a cigarette – it presented a lifestyle to which the male consumer could aspire.

- Pepsi-Cola, always in fierce competition with the leading brand Coca-Cola, broke from its traditional product-oriented brand advertising in 1963 when it ran a contest to come up with a new slogan. The winner: "Come Alive! You're the Pepsi Generation!" A bold campaign was built around the slogan, pitching Pepsi-Cola as a drink for young people and the young at heart, implying that Coca-Cola was old and stodgy. Alan Pottasch, a company executive credited with directing the campaign, said, "For us to name and claim a whole generation after our product was a rather courageous thing that we weren't sure would take off." It took off all right; in fact, the notion of the Pepsi Generation inspired brand advertising well beyond the original campaign. In 1984, Pepsi advertised that it was "the choice of a New Generation," and in 1997, Pepsi promoted "GenerationNext." The "Pepsi Generation" campaign was one of the first to launch a new type of marketing called "lifestyle marketing."

- As indicated earlier, the Volkswagen "Beetle" was originally intended to be a car for the German citizenry during the rise of Nazi Germany. After the war, however, Volkswagen was allowed to remain in business, and the company began to market the unattractive little vehicle to other countries. In the 1950s, it gained popularity with Europeans who found the car appealing because it could handle Europe's narrow roads and it was economical on gas. When the Beetle was introduced in North America, it couldn't immediately compete with the typically larger American models, but it did slowly begin to carve out a market for smaller vehicles. That's when the company made a momentous decision: It gave its modest advertising account to Bill Bernbach, who ran an American ad agency, Doyle Dane Bernbach (DDB).

Before Bernbach started his own firm, he wrote a letter to the management of Grey Advertising, where he worked, in which he urged the agency, "Let us blaze new trails. Let us prove to the world that good taste, good art and good writing can be good selling." They weren't impressed, so he left to start DDB. A proponent of strong creative advertising concepts, Bernbach applied his philosophy to Volkswagen. Everything about the 1960 campaign broke rules, just like the Beetle itself. Unlike the lavishly illustrated full-color magazine ads promoting large American cars, Volkswagen's first ad, done in black-and-white, featured a small photograph of the Beetle shot on a large blank background with the headline, **Think small.** The copy was laid out in three short columns and written in one sentence paragraphs. It described why a small car was better, and ended with the sentence, "Think it over." The Volkswagen logo seemed to be haphazardly positioned within the third column of type. The ad looked nothing like any other automobile ad – but it was authentic, original and different. A subsequent black-and-white ad with the same layout showed a large picture of the Beetle with a one-word headline: **Lemon.** The copy referred to the fact that Volkswagen painstakingly quality controlled every Beetle so that there were no "lemons." The copy ended with the sentence, "We pluck the lemons; you get the plums." Unconventional, genuinely creative advertising served to position a homely little German car as hip and desirable. This campaign is considered one of the best examples of the creative revolution of the 1960s – and a standout in advertising history.

- DDB was behind other notable breakthrough campaigns. Perhaps none was more influential than a single television commercial the agency created on behalf of the 1964 presidential campaign of Lyndon Johnson. The one-minute black-and-white spot showed a beautiful little girl standing in a field, picking petals from a daisy and counting as she dropped each petal to the ground. Suddenly, her counting is replaced with a voiceover countdown (10-9-8-7 etc.) reaching zero and resulting in an atomic bomb explosion. During the explosion, Johnson's voice is heard saying, "These are the stakes: To make a world in which all of God's children can live, or to go into the dark. We must either love each other, or we must die." An announcer ends the commercial with the ominous words, "Vote for President Johnson on November 3. The stakes are too high for you to stay home." This powerful ad was one of the most stunning examples of negative political advertising ever made. The commercial never mentioned Johnson's opponent, Barry Goldwater, but it used a terrifying image to evoke an emotional response and elicit fear about electing him. The ad is credited with branding Goldwater as an extremist and contributing to Johnson winning the presidency. It also had an important, lasting effect on the direction of American political advertising in subsequent years.

These cases – just a handful of excellent brand campaigns – are evidence that some of the most memorable brand advertising in history was executed during this era. When outstanding creativity was combined with audience research and targeting, brand marketing was extremely effective. It is all the more impressive that the brand campaigns developed in the 1960s were highly successful without the media advantage of cable television or the internet.

In an October 3, 2011 article in *The Atlantic*, "How Brands Were Born: A Brief History of Marketing," Marc de Swaan Arons indicates that the leading brands of the 1950s and 1960s "excelled in marketing activities...setting the benchmarks for all brands today." He goes on to write:

> "This marked the start of almost 50 years of marketing where 'winning' was determined by understanding the consumer better than your competitors and getting the total 'brand mix' right. The brand mix is more than logo, or the price of a product. It's also the packaging, the promotions, and the advertising, all of which is guided by precisely worded positioning statements."

America after World War II, leading into the 1950s and 1960s, is a distinctive period in marketing history...when the modern American brand was born.

• A F T E R W O R D •

The Brand Moves On

While I ended the story of American brands in the 1960s, that point in time was really just the start of the modern age of branding. American brands have progressed, becoming a force in both business-to-consumer and business-to-business. Corporate and product brands have developed distinct personalities. Modern brands have the ability to engender remarkable loyalty from consumers. Top brands generate billions of dollars of sales annually and can remain profitable, vibrant and relevant for decades.

Brands have not always had an uncluttered path, however. In the late 1970s and 1980s, when consumers were seeking relief from inflationary prices, the "generic brand" appeared. Unbranded products that attempted to mirror branded products were introduced at value prices. At first, the quality of such products was inferior and consumers were wary, but generics eventually grew into a formidable category all its own. Generics were later joined by "store brands" that were private labeled by large grocery, pharmacy and retail chains. Some packaging even carried promotional messages urging consumers to "compare with [brand name]." This pushed consumer acceptance of generics along the road to mass adoption, putting added pressure on higher priced name brands. Now generics, store brands and private label brands are common; they sit on shelves next to name brands and battle for market share right alongside them.

This is one reason brands have to constantly innovate, both in product development and marketing. They must be tireless in their conviction that buying a branded product is worth it.

Brand marketers have a marketing arsenal available to them that would have been unimaginable in the 1960s. The internet came along and supercharged branding. In addition, there are hundreds of television channels, specialty magazines, websites, social media opportunities, online advertising outlets and e-marketing options. The media landscape has been forever altered. To an unparalleled degree, the brand marketer can today use sophisticated data analysis to identify and target microsegments, cultivate prospects and stay connected to customers. Brands need to use every conceivable marketing weapon to survive, so brand marketing will undoubtedly continue to advance to new levels.

To reach a promising future, brands have continuously evolved. Those brands with lasting legacies were solidly rooted in post-war America.

I hope after reading this book, you have a better appreciation for the rise of the modern American brand.

• SOURCES •

PART I – The American Brand: World War I to World War II

1. How the U.S. Government Branded the Great War

How We Advertised America, George Creel, Harper & Brothers, 1920

https://www.theatlantic.com/business/archive/2014/08/how-advertisers-used-world-war-i-to-sell-sell-sell/375665/

https://en.wikipedia.org/wiki/Propaganda_in_World_War_I

https://dcc.newberry.org/collections/world-war-i-in-us-popular-culture

https://www.pbs.org/wgbh/americanexperience/features/the-great-war-master-of-american-propaganda/

https://illustrationchronicles.com/I-Want-YOU-The-Story-of-James-Montgomery-Flagg-s-Iconic-Poster

https://encyclopedia.1914-1918-online.net/article/graphic_arts_and_advertising_as_war_propaganda

https://www.thedrum.com/news/2014/06/27/world-war-one-propaganda-look-wartime-ads-1914-1918

https://artsandculture.google.com/exhibit/FgIS-a85IVPaLQ

https://www.loc.gov/pictures/collection/wwipos/background.html

2. How American Brands Leveraged the Great War

https://www.history.com/news/world-war-i-inventions-pilates-drones-kleenex

https://www.loc.gov/collections/stars-and-stripes/articles-and-essays/inside-the-pages/advertisements/

https://en.wikipedia.org/wiki/Category:American_companies_established_in_1917

https://commons.wikimedia.org/wiki/Category:1917_advertisements_in_the_United_States

3. American Brands in the 1920s

*Scientific Adverti*sing, Claude Hopkins, Library of Congress, 1923

https://adage.com/article/adage-encyclopedia/history-1920s/98699?

https://en.wikipedia.org/wiki/Category:American_companies_established_in_1920

https://www.history.com/topics/roaring-twenties/roaring-twenties-history

https://brandculture.com/insights/1920s-vs-2020s-a-happy-100-years-to-these-brands/

https://www.khanacademy.org/humanities/us-history/rise-to-world-power/1920s-america/a/1920s-consumption

https://weburbanist.com/2010/06/15/1920s-vintage-ads-marketing-in-a-roaring-post-war-world/

http://www.digitalhistory.uh.edu/disp_textbook.cfm?smtID=2&psid=3396

http://www.eyewitnesstohistory.com/snpmech4.htm

https://sciencestruck.com/inventions-of-1920s

https://www.gilderlehrman.org/history-resources/essays/progressive-era-new-era-1900%E2%80%931929

https://americanhistory.si.edu/collections/search/object/nmah_739493

https://www.history.com/topics/inventions/model-t
https://en.wikipedia.org/wiki/Lucky_Strike

https://en.wikipedia.org/wiki/Coco_Chanel

https://vintage-couture-fashionblog.blogspot.com/2016/06/7-famous-fashion-designers-of-1920s.html

https://www.filmsite.org/20sintro.html

https://www.milwaukeemag.com/story-behind-this-bar-of-palmolive-soap/

https://en.wikipedia.org/wiki/Baby_Ruth

4. American Brands in the 1930s

https://adage.com/article/adage-encyclopedia/history-1930s/98700

https://en.wikipedia.org/wiki/History_of_advertising#On_the_radio_from_the_1920s

https://online.pointpark.edu/public-relations-and-advertising/americas-golden-age-radio/

https://www.encyclopedia.com/social-sciences/culture-magazines/1930s-business-and-economy-overview
https://www.history.com/topics/great-depression/great-depression-history

https://www.forbes.com/2009/04/30/1930s-advertising-innovation-business-supermarket.html#2adb21f1437f

https://en.wikipedia.org/wiki/Category:Products_introduced_in_the_1930s

PART II – The American Brand and World War II

5. At War: Advertising and the U. S. Government

Advertising at War, Inger L. Stole, University of Illinois Press, 2012

All-Out for Victory, John Bush Jones, Brandeis University Press, University Press of New England, 2009

https://scholarship.law.duke.edu/cgi/viewcontent.cgi?article=1940&context=lcp

https://adage.com/article/adage-encyclopedia/war-impact-advertising/98928

https://adage.com/article/75-years-of-ideas/1940s-war-cold-war-consumerism/102702

https://www.nationalww2museum.org/war/articles/world-war-ii-and-popular-culture

https://www.acrwebsite.org/volumes/8204/volumes/v25/NA-25

https://www.nationalgeographic.com/news/2014/12/141207-world-war-advertising-consumption-anniversary-people-photography-culture/

Propaganda/Advertising:
https://en.wikipedia.org/wiki/American_propaganda_during_World_War_II

Founding of Ad Council (War Ad Council):
https://www.adcouncil.org/our-story/our-history

Victory Gardens:
https://www.nytimes.com/2020/07/15/magazine/victory-gardens-world-war-II.html

Rosie the Riveter:
https://www.history.com/topics/world-war-ii/rosie-the-riveter

Women in WWII:
https://www.nationalww2museum.org/war/articles/its-your-war-too-women-wwii

6. World War Brands

Automobile, Tire and Gasoline Brands

https://www.autoweek.com/car-life/classic-cars/a1854671/during-world-war-ii-detroit-car-companies-couldnt-sell-civilian-cars-they-could/

https://www.history.com/news/wwii-detroit-auto-factories-retooled-homefront

https://blog.jeep.com/heritage/the-jeep-brands-role-in-world-war-ii/index.html

Beauty Brands

https://warhawkairmuseum.org/blog/the-patriotism-of-beauty-grooming-fashion-during-wwii/

http://www.oldmagazinearticles.com/WORLD-WAR-2-cosmetic_history#.XxtBLfhKgcg

https://www.upworthy.com/during-wwii-beauty-was-propaganda-but-it-might-ve-helped-win-the-war

Beer Brands

https://www.tandfonline.com/doi/abs/10.2752/175174409X431996

https://vinepair.com/articles/world-war-two-beer-patriotism/

https://www.si.edu/object/advertisement-brewing-industry-foundation:npm_2004.2016.10

http://allaboutbeer.com/article/beer-goes-to-war/

https://eh.net/encyclopedia/a-concise-history-of-americas-brewing-industry/

https://warontherocks.com/2015/06/a-farewell-to-sobriety-part-two-drinking-during-world-war-ii/

https://en.wikipedia.org/wiki/Budweiser

https://www.history.com/this-day-in-history/first-canned-beer-goes-on-sale

https://warontherocks.com/2018/12/how-the-army-made-lager-americas-beer/

Cigarette Brands

http://www.calstatela.edu/sites/default/files/groups/Perspectives/Vol 37/37_blondia.pdf

https://armyhistory.org/reflections-smoke-em-if-you-got-em/

https://en.wikipedia.org/wiki/Lucky_Strike

Railroad Brands

https://www.pullman-museum.org/pshs/pshsFullRecord.php?collection=pshs&pointer=14541

https://blogs.lib.uconn.edu/archives/2019/09/12/the-kid-in-upper-4-a-wartime-advertising-campaign-of-the-new-haven-railroad/

Telephone Brands

https://en.wikipedia.org/wiki/Bell_System

https://www.beatriceco.com/bti/porticus/bell/bellsystem_history.html

https://www.beatriceco.com/bti/porticus/bell/text/western_electric_and_the_bell_system.txt

Bob Hope

https://www.loc.gov/exhibits/bobhope/uso.html#:~:text=World%20War%20II%20Radio%20Broadcast,were%20stationed%2C%20for%20fifty%20years.

http://www.americainwwii.com/articles/bob-hope-and-the-road-to-gi-joe/

https://en.wikipedia.org/wiki/Bob_Hope

Cheerios

https://history.generalmills.com/brand-cheerios.html

https://blog.generalmills.com/2013/07/the-lone-ranger-and-cheerios-long-time-riding-part-ners/#:~:text=General%20Mills%20and%20the%20Lone,millions%20of%20weekly%20radio%20listeners.

https://www.mashed.com/151372/the-untold-truth-of-cheerios/

https://www.mentalfloss.com/article/74142/8-things-you-might-not-know-about-cheerios#

Coca-Cola

https://www.coca-colacompany.com/news/cokes-enduring-legacy-of-inclusive-advertising

https://www.coca-colacompany.com/news/the-chronicle-of-coca-cola-a-symbol-of-friendship#

https://coffeeordie.com/coca-cola-colonels/

http://www.nww2m.com/2011/08/coca-cola-the-pause-that-refreshed-2/

https://www.uso.org/stories/155-the-uso-coca-cola-a-refreshing-75-year-partnership
https://www.warhistoryonline.com/world-war-ii/how-coca-cola-became-the-no-1.html

Disney

https://americanhistory.si.edu/blog/ww2-disney

https://en.wikipedia.org/wiki/Walt_Disney%27s_World_War_II_propaganda_production

https://www.waltdisney.org/wwii

http://www.americainwwii.com/galleries/disney-to-the-front/

https://www.tpr.org/post/when-mickey-went-war

Duck (Duct) Tape

https://www.jnj.com/our-heritage/vesta-stoudt-the-woman-who-invented-duct-tape

https://www.ppmindustries.com/en/news/long-history-duct-tape

https://en.wikipedia.org/wiki/Duct_tape

Florida Citrus Commission

https://americanhomefront.wunc.org/post/frantic-effort-nourish-wwii-troops-led-common-breakfast-staple
https://www.tcpalm.com/story/specialty-publications/your-news/indian-river-county/2016/10/05/vintage-ads-reminder-citrus-importance-during-world-war-ii/91261110/

https://www.navyhistory.org/2014/01/world-war-two-and-the-vitamin-sea-navy-propaganda-posters-of-the-florida-citrus-commission/

Hoover

https://ohiohistorycentral.org/w/Hoover_Company

https://www.thesuburbanite.com/news/20170313/hoover-family-regrets-demise-of-its-iconic-vacuum-business

http://archives.library.wcsu.edu/omeka/files/show/8739

Jeep

https://www.jeep.com/history/1940s.html

https://en.wikipedia.org/wiki/Jeep

https://en.wikipedia.org/wiki/Willys_MB

LIFE

https://archives.library.wcsu.edu/omeka/exhibits/show/world-war-ii-in-life-magazine-/background#

https://en.wikipedia.org/wiki/Life_(magazine)

M&Ms

https://www.militarytimes.com/off-duty/2016/04/14/combat-candy-as-m-ms-turn-75-a-look-at-sweets-in-service/

https://americanhistory.si.edu/blog/chocolate-bars-second-world-war

https://www.confectionerynews.com/Article/2016/11/10/Untold-war-stories-Mars-and-M-M-s-military-history

https://www.huffpost.com/entry/how-world-war-ii-changed-_b_2024730?

Motorola Radio

https://www.motorolasolutions.com/en_xa/about/company-overview/history/explore-motorola-heritage/handie-talkie-radio.html

https://en.wikipedia.org/wiki/SCR-536

https://www.pinterest.com/pin/470063898455193921/

Nash-Kelvinator

http://usautoindustryworldwartwo.com/nash-kelvinator.htm

https://en.wikipedia.org/wiki/Nash-Kelvinator

http://archives.library.wcsu.edu/omeka/exhibits/show/world-war-ii-in-life-magazine-/item/4662

Nescafé

https://www.npr.org/sections/thesalt/2017/04/06/522071853/in-wwi-trenches-instant-coffee-gave-troops-a-much-needed-boost

https://www.nestle.com/aboutus/history/nestle-company-history/nescafe-75-years

Nucoa

http://www.americainwwii.com/articles/victorys-spread/

https://www.soyinfocenter.com/HSS/margarine2.php#:~:text=One%20of%20the%20first%20famous,major%20advance%20in%20product%20quality.

https://www.etsy.com/listing/847691715/1942-nucoa-margarine-print-ad-wwii-era

Nylon

https://www.smithsonianmag.com/arts-culture/stocking-series-part-1-wartime-rationing-and-nylon-riots-25391066/

https://www.smithsonianmag.com/arts-culture/paint-on-hosiery-during-the-war-years-29864389/

Oneida

https://en.wikipedia.org/wiki/Oneida_Limited

https://repousse.wordpress.com/2010/11/09/back-home-for-keeps-oneida-war-time-advertising/

http://www.silvercollection.it/dictionaryADVONEIDAINWWII.html

PB&J

https://whatscookingamerica.net/History/Sandwiches/PeanutButterJellySandwich.htm

https://www.nationalpeanutboard.org/news/who-invented-the-peanut-butter-and-jelly-sandwich.htm

Philco

https://en.wikipedia.org/wiki/Philco

https://philcoradio.com/gallery2/1942b/

http://archives.library.wcsu.edu/omeka/files/show/8639

Raisin Bran

https://www.kelloggs.com/en_US/who-we-are/our-history.html

https://worldhistoryproject.org/1942/kelloggs-raisin-bran-first-available-in-stores

https://northomahahistory.com/2018/11/29/a-history-of-uncle-sam-breakfast-food-company/

Ray-Ban

https://www.businessinsider.com/rayban-military-history-2016-6

https://en.wikipedia.org/wiki/Ray-Ban

RCA

https://collections.ushmm.org/search/catalog/irn619010

https://en.wikipedia.org/wiki/RCA

Silly Putty

https://www.kidsdiscover.com/quick-reads/weird-science-the-accidental-invention-of-silly-putty/

https://www.toyhalloffame.org/toys/silly-putty

SPAM

https://theconversation.com/how-spam-became-one-of-the-most-iconic-american-brands-of-all-time-80030

Superman

https://www.supermanhomepage.com/comics/comics.php?topic=articles/supes-war

https://www.comicmix.com/2009/12/07/how-superman-really-helped-america-win-world-war-two/

https://www.ohiohistory.org/learn/education-and-outreach/in-your-classroom/teachers-toolbox/december-2017/the-creation-of-superman

https://www.sagu.edu/thoughthub/the-political-influence-of-comics-in-america-during-wwii

Westinghouse

https://explorepahistory.com/hmarker.php?markerId=1-A-3A0
https://en.wikipedia.org/wiki/We_Can_Do_It!

https://www.etsy.com/listing/709957044/1943-wwii-westinghouse-electric

Wrigley

https://www.usmintindustry.com/mint-resources/history-of-chewing-gum/

http://www.kration.info/chewing-gum.html

https://en.wikipedia.org/wiki/Wrigley_Company

7. **The Dark Side of World War Brands**

https://www.history.com/news/germany-world-war-i-debt-treaty-versailles

https://allthatsinteresting.com/major-brands-nazi-collaborators

https://www.phactual.com/8-american-companies-that-worked-with-the-nazis-during-world-war-ii/

https://historycollection.com/10-famous-companies-collaborated-nazi-germany/

https://www.bankableinsight.com/companies-that-did-business-with-nazis.html

Chanel

https://www.biography.com/news/coco-chanel-nazi-agent

Chase Bank

https://www.nytimes.com/1998/11/07/world/chase-reviews-nazi-era-role.html

https://en.wikipedia.org/wiki/Chase_Bank#:

Ford

https://www.washingtonpost.com/wp-srv/national/daily/nov98/nazicars30.htm

http://michiganhistory.leadr.msu.edu/wwii-and-ford-motor-company/#

https://www.jta.org/2006/12/06/archive/hitlers-carmaker-part-4-the-last-word-how-will-posterity-remember-general-motors-conduct

General Electric

https://en.wikipedia.org/wiki/General_Electric

http://www.reformation.org/wall-st-ch3.html

https://www.geaviation.com/company/aviation-history

General Motors

https://www.washingtonpost.com/wp-srv/national/daily/nov98/nazicars30.htm

http://usautoindustryworldwartwo.com/generalmotors.htm

https://www.jta.org/2006/12/06/archive/hitlers-carmaker-part-4-the-last-word-how-will-posterity-remember-general-motors-conduct

Hugo Boss

https://en.wikipedia.org/wiki/Hugo_Boss

IBM

IBM and the Holocaust, Edwin Black, Crown, 2001

https://en.wikipedia.org/wiki/Thomas_J._Watson

Kodak

https://en.wikipedia.org/wiki/Kodak

Nestlé

https://www.nestle.com/aboutus/history/nestle-company-history

Siemens

https://new.siemens.com/global/en/company/about/history/company/1933-1945.html

Standard Oil

Sequel to the Apocalypse, John Boylan, Booktab, 1942

https://web.mit.edu/thistle/www/v13/3/oil.html

http://www.reformation.org/wall-st-ch4.html
https://en.wikipedia.org/wiki/Standard_Oil#

Volkswagen

https://www.volkswagenag.com/en/group.html

PART III – The Birth of the Modern American Brand

8. The Consumer in Post-War America

https://www.acrwebsite.org/volumes/8204/volumes/v25/NA-25

https://en.wikipedia.org/wiki/History_of_the_United_States_(1945%E2%80%931964)

https://www.nytimes.com/2020/08/06/opinion/middle-class-prosperity.html?
https://www.history.com/news/post-world-war-ii-boom-economy

https://en.wikipedia.org/wiki/Post–World_War_II_economic_expansion

https://www.loc.gov/classroom-materials/united-states-history-primary-source-timeline/post-war-united-states-1945-1968/overview/

https://en.wikipedia.org/wiki/Category:American_companies_established_in_1946

https://ageofaffluence.weebly.com/consumerism.html

https://www.thoughtco.com/history-of-aerosol-spray-cans-1991231

https://www.plasticstoday.com/business/design-world-war-ii-plastics-and-npe

https://www.history.com/topics/korea/korean-war

The Car Culture

BOOMER BRANDS: Iconic Brands that Shaped Our Childhood, Barry Silverstein, GuideWords Publishing, 2019

BOOMER BRAND WINNERS & LOSERS: 156 Best & Worst Brands of the 50s and 60s, Barry Silverstein, GuideWords Publishing, 2020

9. The Era of Television

The Super Brand Booster

BOOMER BRANDS: Iconic Brands that Shaped Our Childhood, Barry Silverstein, GuideWords Publishing, 2019

BOOMER BRAND WINNERS & LOSERS: 156 Best & Worst Brands of the 50s and 60s, Barry Silverstein, GuideWords Publishing, 2020

https://www.encyclopedia.com/history/culture-magazines/1950s-tv-and-radio#

https://en.wikipedia.org/wiki/History_of_television#United_States

https://en.wikipedia.org/wiki/Amos_%27n%27_Andy

Classic Brands of Early Television

Automobiles and Gasoline

https://adage.com/article/special-report-chevy-100/100-years-chevrolet-advertising-a-timeline/230636

https://www.youtube.com/watch?v=boertpylK0M

https://www.hertz.ca/rentacar/abouthertz/index.jsp?targetPage=CorporateProfile.jsp&c=aboutHertzHistoryView#

https://www.youtube.com/watch?v=p4qslTTVNt4

https://en.wikipedia.org/wiki/Texaco_Star_Theater

https://www.youtube.com/watch?v=b1zxOTDHIBQ

Beauty and Health

https://www.tvdays.com/speedy-alka-seltzer

https://www.legendsofamerica.com/66-burmashave/

https://library.duke.edu/digitalcollections/adviews_american_safety_burma_shave/

https://en.wikipedia.org/wiki/Camay#

https://www.youtube.com/watch?v=lptuVBP05Sg

https://www.leaf.tv/articles/history-of-lifebuoy-soap/

https://www.youtube.com/watch?v=Y4ujmreeO-8

https://americanhistory.si.edu/collections/search/object/nmah_210364#

https://www.youtube.com/watch?v=BEgpFeil4V4

https://www.neotericcosmetics.com/prell-our-story/

https://library.duke.edu/digitalcollections/adviews_prell/

https://www.mum-deo.com/en/story

https://www.youtube.com/watch?v=-EEETMUr8gU&feature=youtu.be

Cereal

https://en.wikipedia.org/wiki/Cocoa_Puffs#

https://www.youtube.com/watch?v=7uVP1Uy5tL0

https://en.wikipedia.org/wiki/Cocoa_Krispies

https://www.dailymotion.com/video/x41fdpt

https://www.insider.com/frosted-flakes-fun-facts-2018-11#frosted-flakes-almost-had-a-kangaroo-mascot-1

https://www.youtube.com/watch?v=YpOZFhas65o

https://en.wikipedia.org/wiki/Maypo#

https://www.youtube.com/watch?v=La1LLDVQ1e8

Cigarettes

https://tobaccocontrol.bmj.com/content/8/1/111

https://en.wikipedia.org/wiki/Kool_(cigarette)#

https://www.youtube.com/watch?v=k1YY5fZtlSM

https://rjrt.com/transforming-tobacco/what-we-make/

https://youtu.be/ch6HafID4DM

https://en.wikipedia.org/wiki/Marlboro_(cigarette)

https://www.youtube.com/watch?v=1TUQ0P-QkpQ
https://www.youtube.com/watch?v=k_klOhy-elo

https://en.wikipedia.org/wiki/Winston_(cigarette)

https://www.youtube.com/watch?v=BVRO6GAfvzA

Cleansers and Detergents

https://en.wikipedia.org/wiki/Ajax_(cleaning_product)#

https://www.youtube.com/watch?v=qFqnGgrilMM

https://en.wikipedia.org/wiki/Ivory_(soap)#

https://www.youtube.com/watch?v=rhBn3xWNQUo

https://en.wikipedia.org/wiki/Mr._Clean
https://www.youtube.com/watch?v=6fg4iTgAvEI

https://www.mrclean.com/en-us/about-mr-clean

https://tide.com/en-us/about-tide/about-us

https://www.youtube.com/watch?v=gMWZWy1rXuY

Convenience Foods

https://en.wikipedia.org/wiki/Clarence_Birdseye

https://www.youtube.com/watch?v=Hd2r3ytr0bg

https://en.wikipedia.org/wiki/Green_Giant

https://www.youtube.com/watch?v=R0LurEEv0lM

https://www.seriouseats.com/2015/08/history-of-jell-o-salad.html

https://www.youtube.com/watch?v=Kj1lXLcklus

https://en.wikipedia.org/wiki/Cheez_Whiz

https://en.wikipedia.org/wiki/Velveeta#
https://en.wikipedia.org/wiki/Kraft_Television_Theatre

https://en.wikipedia.org/wiki/Ovaltine

https://www.youtube.com/watch?v=cocaFUmqfok

https://en.wikipedia.org/wiki/Nesquik

https://www.youtube.com/watch?v=XAqbC9S6U7w

https://en.wikipedia.org/wiki/TV_dinner

https://www.youtube.com/watch?v=49Qn38WdTTs

Fashion

https://fashionhistory.fitnyc.edu/1950-1959/

https://www.liveabout.com/1950s-designers-3420077

https://en.wikipedia.org/wiki/Hush_Puppies

https://www.mlive.com/business/west-michigan/2012/03/hush_puppies_steps_into_mad_me.html

https://www.youtube.com/watch?v=hcPVu0W6T0Q

https://en.wikipedia.org/wiki/Maidenform

http://www.fundinguniverse.com/company-histories/maidenform-inc-history/

https://www.youtube.com/watch?v=ZxXfcdMafYo

https://www.timex.com/the-timex-story/

https://www.youtube.com/watch?v=6EK9KWHjvfM

Music

https://en.wikipedia.org/wiki/Music_history_of_the_United_States_in_the_1950s#

https://en.wikipedia.org/wiki/Chuck_Berry

https://en.wikipedia.org/wiki/The_Dick_Clark_Show

https://en.wikipedia.org/wiki/Elvis_Presley

https://en.wikipedia.org/wiki/Frank_Sinatra

https://en.wikipedia.org/wiki/The_Frank_Sinatra_Show_(1957_TV_series)

https://en.wikipedia.org/wiki/Rat_Pack

Snack Foods

https://www.youtube.com/watch?v=toOMzNXwiQk

https://www.youtube.com/watch?v=QmbelzVP0x4&list=PL2AB267AECDEED56E&index=9

https://www.youtube.com/watch?v=BCc0GlYs05Y

https://www.youtube.com/watch?v=Xw94bqcDUxE

https://us.pez.com/pages/history#

https://www.youtube.com/watch?v=etzla_Hun0Y

https://www.youtube.com/watch?v=yoO9sfbD7DA

Soft Drinks

https://en.wikipedia.org/wiki/RC_Cola

https://en.wikipedia.org/wiki/Diet_Rite

https://en.wikipedia.org/wiki/Kool-Aid

https://www.youtube.com/watch?v=yKY2O4KFmMU

https://www.nesbittsorange.com/facts.htm

https://en.wikipedia.org/wiki/Nesbitt%27s#

Toothpaste

https://www.youtube.com/watch?v=J2gCRIwBq0M

https://www.dailymotion.com/video/x42qsxf

https://en.wikipedia.org/wiki/Pepsodent#

https://www.youtube.com/watch?v=C448gn_RSgI

Toys and Games

https://barbie.mattel.com/en-us/about/our-history.html

https://en.wikipedia.org/wiki/Chatty_Cathy

https://www.youtube.com/watch?v=h8-avPUxyno

https://www.youtube.com/watch?v=f-sYQ8_2v_Q
https://www.toyhalloffame.org/toys/candy-land

https://www.youtube.com/watch?v=4vsZGIrZBuM

https://www.history.com/this-day-in-history/toy-company-wham-o-produces-first-frisbees#

https://www.youtube.com/watch?v=_xyxm4KWHz4

https://en.wikipedia.org/wiki/Hula_hoop

https://www.youtube.com/watch?v=I2gVJT_IcR0

https://en.wikipedia.org/wiki/Toy_train

https://en.wikipedia.org/wiki/Lionel_Corporation

https://www.youtube.com/watch?v=ORADqKuyUKY

10. The Modern Brand is Born

American Business 1920 – 2000: How It Worked, Thomas K. McCraw, Harlan Davidson, 2000

The Hidden Persuaders, Vance Packard, D. McKay Co., 1957

https://hbswk.hbs.edu/archive/american-business-1920-2000-how-it-worked-pg-changing-the-face-of-consumer-marketing

https://www.blueskyeto.com/how-brand-management-changed-since-mad-men-days/

https://en.wikipedia.org/wiki/Rosser_Reeves
https://en.wikipedia.org/wiki/Unique_selling_proposition#

https://en.wikipedia.org/wiki/Vance_Packard

https://www.businessinsider.com/26-sexist-ads-of-the-mad-men-era-2014-5#1950-the-ad-begins-most-husbands-nowadays-have-stopped-beating-their-wives---1

https://youngrestlesscreative.com/2017/02/07/young-restless-creative-in-history-black/

https://www.nytimes.com/2015/04/04/business/media/mad-men-and-the-era-that-changed-advertising.html

The Creative Revolution of the 1960s

https://mascola.com/insights/history-of-advertising-1960s/

https://www.newsweek.com/real-mad-men-behind-60s-ad-revolution-74351

https://www.popneuro.com/neuromarketing-blog/the-black-marlboro-man-history-of-targeted-ads-marketing

https://en.wikipedia.org/wiki/Pepsi_Generation

https://medium.com/theagency/the-ad-that-changed-advertising-18291a67488c

https://en.wikipedia.org/wiki/Volkswagen_advertising

https://www.smithsonianmag.com/history/how-daisy-ad-changed-everything-about-political-advertising-180958741/

https://www.youtube.com/watch?v=riDypP1KfOU

https://www.theatlantic.com/business/archive/2011/10/how-brands-were-born-a-brief-history-of-modern-marketing/246012/

Afterword: The Brand Moves On

https://en.wikipedia.org/wiki/Generic_brand

• APPENDIX •

Print Ads

The Appendix consists of print ads from the World War II era. If an ad is referenced in the text, it is identified by the number below the ad in the Appendix, like this: (*Appendix, 1*). The ad caption will contain information about the advertiser and the year the ad appeared in print. An ad that is not referenced in the text will be explained in that ad's caption.

These ads are included for educational purposes. All of the ads shown appeared without copyright notices when published, so they are assumed to be fair use.

Ads are shown at reduced size and in black-and-white. The original ads were larger and most were full color. The ads have been collected in their original size and color in an online portfolio available to readers of this book. If you would like to receive a link to view the ads online, send your email address to: guidewordspub@gmail.com. In the subject line, please include: **WWB Ads**. Your email will be kept private and not be sold.

1.

U. S. Army, "I Want You for U.S. Army" poster used in both the Great War and World War II (Boston Public Library, licensed under CC BY 2.0)

In wartime as in peace

A special process keeps

KLEENEX

luxuriously soft...
dependably strong!

Your nose knows— there's only one KLEENEX

In your own interest, remember — there is only one *Kleenex*® and no other tissue can give you the exclusive Kleenex advantages!

Because *only Kleenex* has the patented process which gives Kleenex its special softness... preserves the full strength you've come to depend on. And no other tissue gives you the one and only Serv-a-Tissue Box that *never* serves up *just one* double tissue at a time.

That's why it's to your interest not to confuse Kleenex Tissues with any other brand. No other tissue is "just like Kleenex".

In these days of shortages —we can't promise you all the Kleenex you want, at all times. But we do promise you this: *consistent with government regulations*, we'll keep your Kleenex the finest quality tissue that can be made!

There is only one **KLEENEX**
Trade Mark Reg. U.S. Pat. Off.

2.

Kleenex, 1944

3.

Palmolive, 1941

...and make it SNAPPY!

YOU know we're building the biggest army in our history. You know that candy is a fine food for soldiers. Now listen:

"I want millions of special Dextrose energy tablets... millions of candy fruit drops. I want you to package tons of biscuits, bouillon powder, dehydrated mincemeat, prune and apricot powders. I need them... so... *Make it snappy*..."

* * *

This, in effect, is what an aroused War Department told Curtiss Candy Company. We rolled up our sleeves and went to work, just as every other great American company did.

For months our great food plants have been producing and packaging large quantities of food of various kinds. We are operating 24 hours a day.

This service we consider a duty. We are grateful for the opportunity of serving our country in this greatest of all emergencies.

With the Army, the Navy and War Production Plants all calling for Curtiss Products, there may be times when your dealer won't have a complete assortment of Curtiss Candy Bars. But such shortages are only temporary.

If you don't find Baby Ruth or Butterfinger on the candy counter one day — look again the next. We are filling domestic orders as rapidly as our production facilities permit. Every American will agree with us that Uncle Sam comes first!

Here is the Baby Ruth your dealer didn't have yesterday. Occasionally some dealers may temporarily be out of Baby Ruth or Butterfinger. If you don't find them on the counter one day... look again the next. We're doing our best to fill domestic orders... but with us, as with every patriotic American, the boys in service have first call.

BUY U. S. WAR BONDS AND STAMPS

Producers of Fine Foods
CURTISS CANDY COMPANY
CHICAGO, ILLINOIS

4.

Baby Ruth, Curtiss Candy Company, 1943

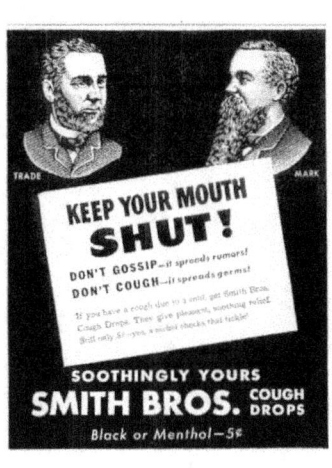

5.

Smith Bros. Cough Drops, 1944

6.

Stetson, 1944

Coty, 1942

8.

Cadillac, General Motors Corporation, 1944

Texaco (The Texas Company), 1943

MORALE IS A LOT OF LITTLE THINGS

There's Bill reading *that letter* again. Want to know what's in it? Well—"Katie had her birthday Thursday ... Dad's an air-raid warden now ... We're going to the football game tomorrow ..."

That's all. Just a letter from the folks. Nothing very important—except to Bill.

But it's important to him all right—the way a lot of little things are to all of us. The letters we get from home ... old friends we meet by chance ... the pipe we smoke in quiet contemplation ...

Little things—but they mean a lot. They chase the blues away ... they help to keep *morale* up!

☆   ☆   ☆

It happens that millions of Americans attach a special value to their right to enjoy a refreshing glass of beer ... in the company of good friends ... with wholesome American food ... as a beverage of moderation after a good day's work.

A small thing, surely—not of crucial importance to any of us. And yet—morale *is* a lot of little things like this. Little things that help to lift the spirits, keep up the courage.

And, after all, aren't they among the things we fight for?

A cool, refreshing glass of beer—a moment of relaxation ... in trying times like these they too help to keep morale up

Brewing Industry Foundation, 1942

11.

Camel, R. J. Reynolds Tobacco Co., 1944

Western Electric, 1942

13.

Bell Telephone System, 1943

14.

Pepsi-Cola, 1942

Florida Citrus Commission, 1943

16.

The Hoover Company, 1943

17.

Willys, 1943

18.

Motorola Radio, Galvin Manufacturing Corporation, 1944

19.

Nash-Kelvinator, 1942

20.

G. Washington's Instant Coffee, 1945

21.

Nescafé, Nestlé, 1945

Nucoa, 1942

23.

Shell Research, 1943 (An ad promoting rayon, a material similar to nylon)

DuPont, 1942 (An ad promoting Cellophane, a DuPont plastic product)

25.

RCA (Radio Corporation of America), 1942 (An ad promoting war bonds and RCA brand radios and phonographs)

26.

NBC (National Broadcasting Company), 1944
(An ad promoting network television)

27.

Lifebuoy, 1942

28.

Mum deodorant, 1945

29.

Kool, 1942

30.

JELL-O, 1945

Ovaltine, 1945

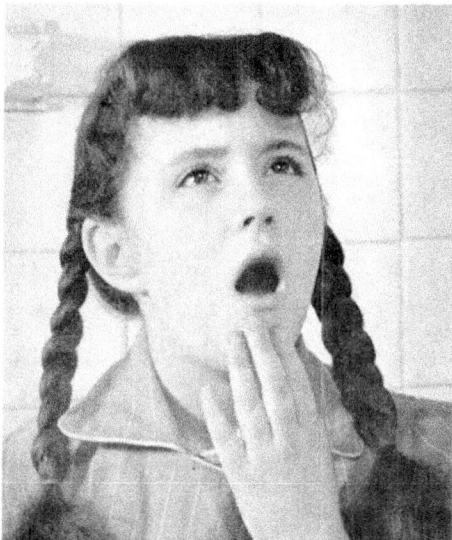

32.

Ipana, 1945

33.

Pepsodent, 1945

34.

H. J. Heinz Company, 1942 (An ad that addresses food shortages)

35.

Mennen, 1942 (An ad that addresses the use of tin for the war effort)

36.

Nestlé's, 1942 (An ad that promotes chocolate as a "fighting food")

37.

Fleischmann's Yeast, 1943 (An ad encouraging Americans to eat bread to help maintain good nutrition)

38.

U. S. Treasury, 1944 (An ad promoting war bonds)

Brand Index

In order to make this index more useful, it is set up in a non-conventional way. Brand references are indexed alphabetically within each chapter rather than as part of a lengthy single list.

Introduction: World War II and American Brands   7
Coca-Cola
Jeep
M&Ms

PART I –
The American Brand: World War I to World War II

1. **How the U.S. Government Branded the Great War**   15

2. **How American Brands Leveraged the Great War**   23
    Aquascutum
    B. F. Goodrich
    Burberry
    Detroit Electric
    Fatima
    Gillette
    Kleenex
    Kotex
    Lucky Strike
    Pompeian Night Cream

3. **American Brands in the 1920s**   31
    Ace Hardware
    Birds Eye
    Carvel
    Chrysler

CVS
Delta Air Lines
Hasbro
Howard Johnson's
Lowe's
Metro Goldwyn Mayer
Pan American Airways
Radio Shack
Rubbermaid
Schick
7-Eleven
Thom McAn
The Walt Disney Company
Wise Foods

4. **American Brands in the 1930s**   37
Alka-Seltzer
Bisquick
Chex
Friskies
Fritos
Hawaiian Punch
Jiffy
Kahlua
King Kullen
Kodachrome
Kool
Kroger
Lays
Lestoil
Miracle Whip
Nescafé
Old Spice

Ritz
Scotch Tape
Skippy
Snickers
Spam
Tampax
Titleist
Tums
Twinkies
V8
View-Master
Windex

PART II –
The American Brand and World War II

5. At War: Advertising and the U.S. Government — 43
Betty Crocker
Birds Eye
Borden
Coty
General Mills
Goodyear
Green Giant
Libbey-Owens-Ford
Lucky Strike
Smith Bros.
Stetson
Timken

6. World War Brands   59

American Motor Car (AMC)
AT&T
Bell System
Blue Bonnet
Bob Hope
Budweiser
Cadillac
Camel
Cheerios
Chesterfield
Chrysler
Coca-Cola
Cocoa Puffs
Disney
Doublemint
Duck Tape
Elizabeth Arden
Ford
FORTUNE
General Mills
General Motors (GM)
General Tire
Hershey
Hoover
Ivory
Jeep
Kix
Kellogg
LIFE
Lucky Strike
Max Factor
M & Ms

WORLD WAR BRANDS

Motorola
Nash-Kelvinator
NECCO
Nescafé
Nestlé
New Haven Railroad
Nucoa
Nylon
Old Gold
Oldsmobile
Oneida
Palmolive
Parkay
Pepsi-Cola
Pepsodent
Peter Pan
Philco
Pontiac
Pullman
Ray-Ban
RCA
RCA Victor
Schlitz
Silly Putty
Skippy
SPAM
Superman
Texaco
Texas Oil Company
TIME
Trix
Western Electric
Westinghouse

White-Westinghouse
Willys-Overland
Wonder
Wrigley

7. **The Dark Side of World War Brands**   109
Associated Press
Bayer
BMW
Chanel
Chase
Coca-Cola
Esso/Exxon
Fanta
Ford
General Electric (GE)
General Motors (GM)
Hugo Boss
IBM
Kodak
Nestlé
Siemens
Standard Oil
Volkswagen (VW)

PART III –
The Birth of the Modern American Brand

8. **The Consumer in Post-War America**   131
American Express
Bank Americard
Cadillac
Carte Blanche

Chevrolet (Chevy)
Corvette
Diner's Club
Edsel
Ford
GM
GTO
MasterCard
Mustang
Nylon
Thunderbird
Tupperware
VISA

9. **The Era of Television** 145
Ajax
Alka-Seltzer
Ban
Barbie
Birds Eye
Burma-Shave
Camay
Candy Land
Chatty Cathy
Cheez Whiz
Chevrolet
Chuck Berry
Cocoa Krispies
Cocoa Puffs
Colgate
Crest
Diet Rite

Drake's
Elvis Presley
E-Z Pop
Frank Sinatra
Frisbee
Frosted Flakes
General Electric
General Mills
General Motors
Green Giant
Halo
Hertz
Hostess
Hula Hoop
Hush Puppies
Ipana
Ivory Snow
JELL-O
Jiffy Pop
Kool
Kool-Aid
Kraft Singles
Lifebuoy
Lionel
Maidenform
Marlboro
Maypo
Mr. Clean
Mum
Nesbitt's Orange
Nestlé's Quik
Nesquik

Newport
Ovaltine
Pepsodent
PEZ
Philco
Playtex
Pontiac
Post
Prell
RC Cola
Rice Krispies
Secret
Swanson
Texaco
Tide
Timex
Velveeta
Winston

10. The Modern Brand is Born — 185

Alcoa
Chase & Sanborn
Lyndon Johnson
Marlboro
Pepsi-Cola
Van Heusen
Volkswagen

About the Author

Barry Silverstein is a brand historian, freelance writer and retired direct marketing/brand marketing professional. He founded and ran his own direct marketing agency for twenty years and has forty-plus years of marketing experience. He is the author of numerous non-fiction marketing/small business books and eGuides, including BOOMER BRANDS, BOOMER BRAND WINNERS & LOSERS and The Breakaway Brand.

Visit his website: https://www.barrysilverstein.com

About the Publisher

GuideWords Publishing publishes books about Boomers, brands and small business. Other books you may enjoy: Let's Make Money, Honey: The Couple's Guide to Starting a Service Business, BOOMER BRANDS and BOOMER BRAND WINNERS & LOSERS.

To learn more about our books, visit our website: https://www.guidewordspub.com

Did you enjoy reading this book?

Word of mouth is so important to a book's ability to reach the right audience. If you enjoyed reading WORLD WAR BRANDS, I hope you will consider recommending it to family, friends, and any World War II or brand enthusiasts you know. A positive online review would also be very much appreciated.

Thank you!
Barry Silverstein
https://www.barrysilverstein.com

www.ingramcontent.com/pod-product-compliance
Lightning Source LLC
Chambersburg PA
CBHW070532010526
44118CB00012B/1105